HIGHLY
SENSITIVE

2 Books in 1: Empathy Survival Guide +
Mindfulness Meditation for Beginners.
Learn How to Control Your Emotions,
Reduce Anxiety And Protect Yourself in
Toxic Relationship

Deniel Clark

Table of Contents

Empath Survival Guide

Description 14

Introduction 17

What is an Empath? 17

CHAPTER 1 20

Are you an empath? 20

Do you walk into markets and feel overwhelmed?
.... 20

Do you meet people and immediately recognize
something personal about them that they have
never told you? 20

Do you meet someone and instantly become
unwell? 21

Did you witness any strange phenomena as a
child? 21

Do you sense the energy emitted by buildings? .21

Do people call you antisocial? 22

Do you notice the small things? 22

Can you read people's minds? 22

Do other people open up to you quite easily? 23

Are you good at bursting liars? 23

Do your friends complain that you are too
sensitive? 23

Are you awesome at spotting fake people? 24

Are you particularly compassionate? 24

Do you experience another person's feelings as if
they were your own? 24

Do you become ill when you spend time with ill
people? 25

Do you love animals deeply? 25

Are you a loner? 26

Are you creative? Fantasize a lot? 26

Do you see visions and revelations in your
dreams? 27

Are you allergic to loud noise? 27

Do animals flock to you? 28

Do you have weird tastes in fashion and entertainment? 28

CHAPTER 2: 30

The Gift of Being an Empath.................................. 30

Responsibilities 35

CHAPTER 3 39

Empath Weaknesses.. 39

Attracting Narcissistic People 40

Knowing Better but Not Doing Better 42

Taking on Responsibilities that Aren't Yours..... 43

Struggling to Live a "Normal" Life 45

Difficulty with Routines..................................... 46

Weak Boundaries..47

The tendency to Have Addictions....................... 48

CHAPTER 4 50

Understanding and Controlling Your Emotions....... 50

Use Your Body Language....................................53

Use Positive Thinking..55

Use Positive Speaking..57

Create Your Own Personal Space.......................59

Work on Time Management 62

CHAPTER 5:...65

Raising Empathetic Children..............................65

CHAPTER 6 71

Empathy in Your Relationships 71

The real problem is this. 71

The empath can get moody. 72

Inconsistency could create more struggles. 73

Empaths are able to pick up on complacency. 73

Empaths can't give up. 74

Empaths like their own space, but don't like being
alone...74

They don't get taken seriously.............................75

Relationship Sabotage 76

CHAPTER 7:... 80

How Empaths Can Understand and Help Other

People 80

CHAPTER 8 85

Energy Vampires and Psychic Attacks 85

    Different types of energy vampires. 85

    The Reasons Behind Vampirism & Narcissism 89

    How to deal with energy vampires. 91

CHAPTER 9 97

Cleansing Negative Energies 97

CHAPTER 10 109

Setting Energetic Boundaries 109

    How To Set Boundaries 111

    Breathing Techniques For Protection 115

    Tips For Setting Boundaries 119

    Empath Meditation 119

    Scan and Check 120

    Mantra 121

    Block or not? 121

CHAPTER 11: 123

Overcoming Your Fears, Grasping Your Power, And Nurturing Your Empathic Abilities 123

The Benefits of Nurturing Your Inner Empath. 124

Learning to Overcome Fears 126

How to Nurture Your Gift for a Better Life 129

Seek Positive Experiences and People in Your Life
....130

CHAPTER 12: 135

Empathic Self-Care Tips 135

Re-Charge Often 136

Exercise Your Creativity 137

Consider Working for Yourself 138

Practice Energy Clearing Often 140

Meditate 140

Hot Showers 141

Himalayan Salt Baths 141

Binaural Beats 142

CHAPTER 13 151

Exercises for Empaths 151

   Meditation 153

   Realigning Energies 156

   Connecting to the Earth 158

   Self-Care 160

   Creating Boundaries 163

   Putting Yourself First 165

Conclusion 167

Table of Contents

Mindfulness Meditation for Beginners

Description 169

Introduction 171

Getting started 172

History of Meditation 178

Benefits of Mindfulness 182

Benefits to Mental Health 183

Benefits of Different Forms of Mindfulness 193

Medical forms of Mindfulness 194

Benefits of Mindfulness Meditation for Children: 202

Cognitive Benefits 203

Social Benefits 204

Emotional Benefits 204

Benefits of Mindfulness Meditation for Teenagers: 206

Techniques to Practice Mindfulness Meditation 212

Technique #1 –Mindfulness Meditation through Simple Breathing 212

Technique #2 –Mindfulness Meditation through Concentrated Breathing 214

Technique #3 – Mindfulness Body Scan

Meditation 218

Technique #4 – Mindfulness Meditation through Mantra Chanting 220

Technique #5 – Mindfulness Meditation while Walking 222

Technique #6 – Mindfulness Meditation through an Empty Mind 225

Technique #7 – Mindfulness Meditation through Observations 227

Technique #8 – Mindfulness Meditation for Increased Awareness 228

Technique #9 – Mindfulness Meditation in Conversations 230

Technique #10 – Mindfulness Meditation through Appreciation 234

Declutter Your Mind 238

Anxiety Mindfulness Meditation 248

Mindfulness Meditation Script For Anxiety #1 248

Mindfulness Meditation For Anxiety #2 251

Meditation and stress reduction 260

What is Meditation? 260

How Meditation Helps Reduce Stress and Anxiety 261

Let me elaborate on that with an example. 261

Benefits of Meditation 268

1: Reduces Stress 268

2: Can Improve Your Sense of Wellbeing 269

3: Can Improve Your Sense of Empathy, Connectedness, and Relationships 270

4: Can Improve Your Focus 270

5: Can Unlock Your Creative Side 271

6: Can Help You Overcome Addictions 271

7: Can Improve Your Decision Making Skills ... 271

8: Can Strengthen Your Heart and Improve Your Health 272

How Meditation Works 273

Different Kinds of Meditation 280

Chanting Meditation 280

Mindfulness Meditation 284

Focused Meditation 286

Walking meditation 289

Meditation in the workplace and while traveling 291

Keeping up the motivation 294

How to prepare for meditation 297

Pick a Nice Spot 297

Choose a Time of the Day You're Free 299

Wear Comfortable Clothes 299

Keep a Timer.. 300

Get a Zafu 300

Comfortable Pose 301

Mindful Meditative Practice and Simple Exercise
Examples 305

Cultivating Mindfulness into daily life 321

    Tip #1: The Power of the Morning Ritual 321

    Tip #2: Keep it Short and Sweet 322

    Tip #3: Create Effective Cues 323

    Tip #4: Weave it into existing routines 325

    Tip #5: Cut Down Options 326

Conclusion 328

Empath Survival Guide

The Complete Strategies For Highly Sensitive People. Learn to Manage Your Emotions, Overcome Anxiety, protect yourself in Toxic Relationship from Narcissists and Energy Vampires

Deniel Clark

Description

Empaths are said to be "poets in motion." They see the world in a wonderfully creative and artistic way. They are generally highly artistic, creating art in every way imaginable. Some may master a particular art form, whereas others may prefer to dabble in a little bit of everything. Empaths see the world in a way that most others don't. To them, each day is a new chapter, and the book needs to be written in the most poetic way possible.

An Empath can be virtually anyone. They are not known to be isolated to any particular gender, race, culture, or religion. Empaths exist anywhere and everywhere. With the help of this guide, you will learn the following:

- What is an Empath?

- How to know if you are an Empath

- The Gift of Being an Empath

- Empath Weaknesses

- Understanding and Controlling Your Emotions

- Raising Empathetic Children

- Empathy in Your Relationships

- Energy Vampires and Psychic Attacks

- Cleansing Negative Energies

- Setting Energetic Boundaries

- Overcoming Your Fears, Grasping Your Power, And Nurturing Your Empathic Abilities

- Self-Care Tips and Exercises

If you are an Empath, who aspires to be successful in any area of your life – congratulations! You have the immensely valuable combination of the right skills and mindset required to rise to the top in whatever you set your mind to. By following the steps outlined in this book, you will be able to control your energy, whether it is by refilling your energy reserves, preventing negative energy from getting to you in the first place, or simply getting rid of any clutter which has accumulated within your mind for a period of time.

Thanks for downloading this book. It's my firm belief that it will provide you with all the answers to your questions.

Introduction

Empaths are a form of highly sensitive individuals that are known for being able to experience the energies of other individuals energetically. Rather than simply experiencing the emotion of empathy, Empaths can emotionally, mentally, and physically sense and feel another person's experience. This enables Empaths to be highly sensitive toward other people. This is both a curse and a blessing, depending on how it is used and cared for by the Empath themselves.

What is an Empath?

An Empath is said to be a person who has a paranormal ability to actually "step into" the state of another individual. Empaths are highly sensitive beings who can literally sense and feel the emotions and feelings of other individuals. If an individual is an Empath, they can sense deep emotions beyond what someone else is actively expressing. This means even if an individual is highly gifted at hiding their emotions or masking them with other emotions, an

Empath can sense, feel, and intricately understand the true emotions of that individual. Not only can the Empath sense and feel these emotions, but they can also understand them on a deep level.

Empaths have the capacity to experience complete empathy toward virtually anyone and everyone else. They can sense it towards family, friends, associates, kids, strangers, animals, plants, and even inanimate objects. Some people are known to be more empathetic toward certain things over others. This is often how we end up with things like "animal whisperers" or "plant whisperers." When this happens, that particular person is known to be more empathetic toward that which they can supposedly "whisper" to. What is really happening is not a whisper, but instead a deep inner knowing of what the other's needs are.

If a person is an Empath, they are not restricted by time and space. In fact, they are not really restricted at all. An Empath can sense the emotions and mental state of people who are incredibly far away. Some can even sense the emotions and mental state of individuals who have long since passed. For example, if they were to visit a museum and see the belongings of someone who existed many years ago but who has since passed away, some Empaths can step directly into the feelings and energies of that person. This enables Empaths to be deeply understanding and to have a highly unique perspective of the world around them.

CHAPTER 1:

Are you an empath?

The following questions are designed to make you eliminate doubt that you are indeed an empath.

Do you walk into markets and feel overwhelmed?
For most people, walking to the market is a seemingly enjoyable thing, but when it comes to an empath, they might become terrified of it. This is because walking in the market will bring them into contact with many people, and considering their ability to absorb other people's energies, they will have a hard time of it as they absorb the (mostly) negative energies of other people.

Do you meet people and immediately recognize something personal about them that they have never told you?
Some empaths have intuitive power that shows them even hidden stories about certain people. For such people, they will meet someone and then become

aware of something that no one has ever shared with them. It may seem as though they are dreaming or out of their minds, but they very sober and their intuition is on point.

Do you meet someone and instantly become unwell? Empaths are highly sensitive individuals, and they can usually perceive someone who means to harm others.

Did you witness any strange phenomena as a child? Most empaths report having seen some weird phenomena like ghosts, alien ships, angels, and imaginary friends that they even held conversations with. Empaths tend to have a mysterious life that they never reveal to most people.

Do you sense the energy emitted by buildings?
An empath can be able to tell whether a building has bad or good energy. They are intrinsically aware of how good buildings differ from bad ones. Also, empaths can perceive the energies of the latest inhabitants of a building and use that as a gauge.

Do people call you antisocial?

If you have seen someone go without friends for the longest time, there's a chance that that person is an empath. The empath wants to have a tight-knit group of friends, but not socialize as a big group. This is because socializing in groups exposes the empath to the energies of many different people which drains them of energy.

Do you notice the small things?

Most people tend to notice superficial qualities either in things or other people, but an empath goes a step further; noticing the particulars. For instance, an empath will not only remember that you had a pocket square, but also it's color, the style you had used, and exactly where it was pinned.

Can you read people's minds?

An empath could be speaking with someone and see the range of things that the other person is thinking about but not saying. If the other person is putting on a pretentious face, the empath will still know.

Empaths have an innate ability to sniff out people who

that like pretending.

Do other people open up to you quite easily?
For the most part, an empath minimizes their interaction with other people. But when they decide to socialize, they find that they are magnets for people that are looking for a savior. People seem to think that empaths have the answers.

Are you good at bursting liars?
An empath doesn't have to follow around someone in order to be sure that they are telling lies or the truth. All an empath needs to do is take one long look into your eyes and decide whether you are telling the truth or lies. Empaths tend to catch a lot of people telling lies, unnecessary lies, and the empaths are usually not amused. It worries them.

Do your friends complain that you are too sensitive?
You have been a sensitive kid since you were a little person. There are many things, mostly negative, that stimulate you. For instance, a violent TV scene could wreck your mood. The pronouncement of a wrong

word could shock you.

Are you awesome at spotting fake people?
An empath is good at sniffing people who are trying to be what they are not. They can perceive the emotional and mental makeup of this fakes. An empath tends to get frustrated by such people because they are liars and also not very creative.

Are you particularly compassionate?
Compassion is a rare quality among humans. But empaths seem to be another species altogether for their compassion knows no bounds. They will stop to help anything or anyone that is in need. Empaths seem to hope that other people can be compassionate too, but they end up frustrated.

Do you experience another person's feelings as if they were your own?
This is the classic quality of an empath. For instance, an empath could be seated alone, enjoying their favorite movie, enjoying a balanced emotional state. Then someone else joins them, and all hell goes loose.

Shortly after, the empath starts to experience violent thoughts, and they are confused as to what just happened. It's simple. The empath started drawing the violent feelings of the person next to them, thus ruining their emotional stability.

Do you become ill when you spend time with ill people?

Not all empaths are like this, but there's a category of empaths that typically get sick when they surround themselves with sick people. These empaths have the ability to pick up the symptoms of the ill people around them and then manifest these symptoms as if they were their own.

Do you love animals deeply?

The average Joe on the street might own a pet and say things like, "O, I love Miky!" most people have a shallow relationship with their pets. But the case is totally different where empaths are concerned.

Empaths have a deep liking for animals that they can almost communicate in their own strange ways. When an empath hears stories of animal cruelty, their heart breaks into a million shards. Empaths are committed toward fighting for animal rights.

Are you a loner?

Just because someone is a loner doesn't mean that he is an empath, and vice versa is true. In modern societies, being a loner is sort of looked down upon. People wonder why loners can't seem to get friends and then conclude that something must be wrong with them. Being a loner also means that you have got to be treated as a threat. People are not done with you yet, and they seem to think that you are up to no good. Empaths are actually happy to be loners, considering that they like spending time alone.

Are you creative? Fantasize a lot?

Many empaths are already disappointed with what the planet had to offer (violence and more bullshit). They found it easier to retreat to their caves and find something else to do. They find themselves in a creative space, and they begin to create fantasies. And this offers them a window of escape. Empaths tend to be extremely creative people, and their fantasies are pretty wild.

Do you see visions and revelations in your dreams? Some empaths have the gift of telling what the future will be like. These empaths receive their revelations through various means, especially dreams, and visions. Sometimes the dreams and visions can be literal, and sometimes they are euphemistic and must be broken down into simple language. Either way, the empath is up to the task. Most of what empaths predict usually comes to pass.

Are you allergic to loud noise?
It may seem like something trivial for an empath to be allergic to, but when a blaring car passes by, or when someone decides to let the whole neighborhood know that their daddy has bought a new speaker, the empath will react with a sharp scream of pain, expressing shock and discomfort. And then whoever is behind that deafening noise – if they are knowable – is entered into the empath's book of mortal enemies. Seriously though, nothing scares an empath more than sudden, excessive noise.

Do animals flock to you?

Animals also have a very sensitive internal locator for their friends. When coming upon empaths, they can tell for the fact that they have met true friends. You will find dogs and cats always coming up to the empath and trying to get their attention. They feel so secure and loved when they are around an empath.

Do you have weird tastes in fashion and entertainment?

Ask a random person who's their favorite artist, and they will drop the name of a familiar, internationally acclaimed artist. But then ask an empath the same question, and their answer might baffle you: someone you have never heard about, and who does some weird things with even weirder instruments. The thing about empaths is that they stand out even when they are not trying to draw any attention to themselves.

Empaths project their difference through their unusual wishes, likes, and interests. When the average person is interested in the most mainstream entertainer or a successful franchise, expect the empath to have their own version of whom they consider to be the best singer or entertainer, or what they consider to be the best movie, and it will surely defy the conventional standards. Empaths break the norms even when they don't mean to. They are just different, and they are not trying to pull an act.

CHAPTER 2:

The Gift of Being an Empath

Being an empath is a wonderful gift. When you are able to handle this gift correctly, it will give you a very satisfying and pleasant life. It is estimated that about 2% of the population anywhere have empath abilities. This makes us quite special, indeed.

Empaths have the ability and potential to help people around them. They are able to not only feel the emotions of people around them but to also understand what is going on. A person close to them may be having some difficulty in life, but they may not be able to pinpoint the cause of that difficulty correctly. An empath may be able to understand the person and the problem better. The empath can then offer some guidance as to how such a person can overcome their problems.

There are many ways empaths can take advantage of the gift by helping others. They could make great counselors or behavioral coaches or psychologists.

Empaths can also excel in many other areas. For instance, in sports, which involves a lot of strategies and tactics, empaths can use their ability to second-guess opponents' future moves. In team sports such as soccer, empaths would make great playmakers who can help dictate the gameplay and come up with winning moves.

Empaths see the world differently than most other people. They care about the well-being of people not only around them but also those far away. They can easily empathize with people who come from different socio-economic backgrounds. Empaths can make wonderful social activists or politicians.

The world is constantly in flux. The social and political landscape is changing for the better most of the time, but other times, they are changing for the worse. People are becoming more aware of the surrounding environment. Politics is slowly becoming a noble field again after it became the domain of greed and authoritarianism. There will be greater demand for compassionate leaders rather than pliable puppets running errands for the rich few rather than the many. There is certainly a place for empaths in this field. Being able to feel and understand the needs of the masses—regardless of class, age, gender, or ethnicity—is something that empaths certainly have. Empaths always seek to understand things on a deeper level. They are able to see and understand multiple different points of views. In a particular global conflict, they have the ability to help people solve conflicts because they can understand what the root of the problem is and because they understand what the needs and motivations of each party to the conflict are. For example, the conflict surrounding Syria is a complex situation with many different factions. It becomes more complicated with the involvement of neighboring countries and other international powers. The situation has become so convoluted that sometimes groups who were initially enemies have found themselves to be in the same faction.

The world is moving towards uncharted territory. The human population has been rising exponentially consistent with the pace of development and technology. Unexpected challenges are always around the corner—for example, global warming. Humans have been enjoying all the benefits that the earth has to offer. It has given us life, energy, and much more—but right now, the earth is slowly feeling the effects of unrestrained human economic activities. Everyone has to find a way to reverse this damage. Empaths can play a role to feel the earth's vibrations and understand its needs and help it heal. And in spite of all this, global superpowers are still more interested in the accumulation of wealth and power. The situation appears to be better now than it is in the past, and we are grateful for it. However, the tendency for greed and distrust is still present and strong. Some governments busy themselves starting conflicts around the world. Some are itching to start a global war, threatening other nations with nuclear weapons. Governments are powerful entities. They are supposed to represent the collective people of the land they control. Therefore, they ought to also behave humanely. They need to have more compassion and empathy. We can help contribute to this change by spreading love, empathy, and promoting mutual understanding. There are, of course, already people working towards this goal, but they seriously need all the help they could get. We do not need to go against the powerful forces to achieve our goal. We just need to spread the love and healing as much and as far wide as we can.

At the present time, there are so many unsolved issues in this world if we look beyond our own safe bubble. At the same time, we are slowly moving towards evolution in terms of human consciousness. Empaths have the potential to be one of the leading catalysts ushering humanity into a new dawn.

In no way is this book pressuring the empaths to take on this huge responsibility; it is only if you see this as an opportunity, then it will be a worthwhile course of action to take. Always remember to keep in check our own vulnerabilities and limits. The main point of this book is to serve as a guide as to how to handle our condition. Most of us would probably have only recently discovered that we are empaths and are more likely still having difficulties coping with it.

A final thing to note is never to let pride get the better of you. There may be some empaths who may think that being empaths makes us special in the sense of being better than other people. Do not entertain such thoughts if you ever found it tempting enough. Many empaths have fallen into this trap. When excessive pride is combined with certain childhood trauma, this may result in a special form of introverted narcissism, sometimes referred to as covert narcissism.

Responsibilities

Like any gift or power in the world, there is a responsibility attached to these abilities. We have already mentioned about the responsibility to protect ourselves from unwanted energies in the world.

Besides that, there are other responsibilities we should also consider. One of them is the responsibility to use our ability for the good of all. The gift should never be used for the harm or trouble of other beings. When we are comfortable enough with our abilities, the best thing we can do is to heal. We can heal people, animals, earth, plants, etc. We also have a task to share our abilities and share our insights. Empaths are given access to things which many people cannot see or feel or even fathom. We are given deep insights into the bigger picture, the state of things, or the way the future is going to be played. We should share it as far as we think it is necessary. Empaths should never use our abilities to use whatever details we may have caught on and to use it for self-gratification and to the detriment of the other person. We have a duty to continue having compassion towards others. When we put up our energy shields, it does not mean that we are shutting everyone out, or shutting ourselves in.

This is just a means of protecting our selves. We will continue to help others as best as we can. We cannot forget this. With the shield, we are just controlling the flow of energies and protecting ourselves from harm.

If we are nature empaths, we have a responsibility to

continue listening in on the planet. Making sure she is doing fine. And if not, we should find a way to help her. If we can't make others change, then we have to be the change that is needed. I know this sounds like a really big responsibility. Of course, this is optional. It can be taken up by the most energetic or expert level empaths.

Parents of empaths carry a big burden too. If the parent is also an empath, then it will be a lot easier. If you are not an empath but are reading this, then surely you are not sociopathic or such and therefore would have some empathy. The child will have to face steep difficulties growing up. They may have trouble fitting in in school, and elsewhere. Do not ever create a situation where the child could not even fit in at home. The home is the child's home. Guide them from there. However, do not be too worried. Children are more resilient than we always thought. They can repair more easily than adults. At least they have that. And they may continue having issues after growing up. That is quite normal. Continue helping them through difficult changes in life. They will need all the help they can get.

Empaths also have a responsibility to help other empaths, especially newly realized empaths. There may be empaths who are having more difficulty dealing with empathic issues. People are not all wired the same way. Some empaths may have begun with negative energy or naturally has a lot of negative emotions around themselves. We should help them out whenever we can and help them channel that negative energy away. Some empaths may continue to live in denial, refusing to accept their nature due to some personal reasons of their own. If you feel that they might have a need for your help, then, by all means, go ahead and help them.

CHAPTER 3:

Empath Weaknesses

"We are a slave to our emotions when we don't acknowledge or fear their teachings – be brave through empathy."

Christel Broederlow

As with anything, Empaths also have weaknesses. The weaknesses you face may be debilitating for you, depending on how much you experience them.

Unfortunately, most Empaths are not aware of what they are, so they end up going through life living in fear of their weaknesses. This prevents them from developing their strengths and can result in them feeling overburdened by their gift. Trust that if you recognize or relate to any of these weaknesses, recognizing them and giving yourself the space to come to terms with them is important. This is where you can begin to heal them and step into your power. As a result, you can keep your weaknesses in check as you give yourself the space required to develop your strengths. Then, a natural balance will arise, and you will have the opportunity to live a life in alignment with your gift.

Attracting Narcissistic People

One unfortunate weakness of Empaths, even stronger ones, is attracting narcissistic people into their lives. Although you might feel intolerant toward narcissists, you may also find yourself overly surrounded by them. The reason why this happens is simple: you have the one thing they lack. Empathy.

Narcissists are drawn to people who have excess empathy because they can exploit that empathy to get what they want. They also love people who have a low sense of self-worth and low self-esteem. If you are not careful, they can exploit you to have their own selfish needs met. This can result in Empaths finding themselves trapped in narcissistic relationships that drain them of their energy and cause them to feel overwhelmed and taken advantage of. Unfortunately, because you can see from the other person's perspective and many narcissists are believed to be narcissistic as a result of childhood trauma, this can result in you siding with the narcissist. Your desire to heal others may result in you attempting to save someone who cannot be saved. That is unless they choose to save themselves.

If you find yourself being surrounded by narcissists or recognize narcissistic relationships presently or previously in your life, this is likely because of the fact that you are Empathic. When not properly protected, you can easily be disillusioned by narcissists who can result in a lot of trauma in your own life.

It is important to understand that even if you are finding yourself surrounded by narcissists, there is a way to protect yourself and you are not doomed to be abused and hurt by narcissists for your entire life. As you strengthen your protection abilities, self-worth, self-care, and heal from your mistrust in yourself and your inner voice, you will begin to find it easier for you to identify and recognize a narcissist. Then, you can avoid them in favor of healthier relationships.

Knowing Better but Not Doing Better

Empaths have a tendency to know better but not actually do better. This is not because they don't want to do better, but because they are conditioned to think of themselves as "wrong." Through bullying, societal conditioning, and other abandonment in childhood and young adulthood, Empaths are taught that their inner knowingness is false and that they should not believe it. This causes doubt in the Empaths intuition. If this has happened to you, you might find it difficult to trust and act on your inner knowingness. As a result, you may find yourself missing out on opportunities or kicking yourself for not acting sooner. This is extremely common. Feeling like you should have acted sooner because "you knew better" is a really common feeling for Empaths.

It is important to note that until now, even if you did know better, you didn't do better because you genuinely couldn't. Your conditioning resulted in you feeling and believing that you were truly unable to act on what you felt you knew. As a result, you did not act.

This is not your fault. If this is something you face, healing your trust in yourself, your intuition and strengthening your sense of self-worth and self-confidence will help you in believing your gut reaction and feeling confident in your inner knowingness.

Then, you can begin knowing and doing better. You may end up feeling like you are living in greater alignment with yourself and you will have fewer instances of feeling like "I shouldn't have done that!" or "I should have done this!"

Taking on Responsibilities that Aren't Yours
As an Empath, you may find yourself taking on responsibilities that are not yours. Empaths have a sense of duty that is hard for them to avoid. Knowing things on a deeper level leads to you feeling like it is your responsibility to do the things that others are not doing. This is because you feel that if you don't, no one will. You may find yourself struggling to balance too many responsibilities, many of which are not rightfully yours. Many Empaths report feeling like they are "carrying the weight of the world on their

shoulders" when they experience these symptoms.

Taking on these responsibilities can manifest on a personal level, a collective level, or both. You may find yourself taking on other people's responsibilities directly in your life. For example, at work, you may realize that people are not doing their complete jobs because of personal struggles. As a result, you take on their responsibilities for them. This can be kind, but it can also lead to you being overwhelmed and taken advantage of. You may also find this happening in other areas of your life as well. Many Empaths take on the responsibilities of others and become taken advantage of, by anyone from friends and family, to coworkers and even parents of other children if you are a parent yourself. It is important to know that you still need to put yourself first. Helping people is great, but you still need to keep a balance in your life and establish healthy boundaries.

On a collective level, Empaths may take on more responsibility by feeling like it is their duty to heal the world of major tragedies. For example, you may find yourself feeling as though you are personally responsible for healing world hunger, ending the war, or finding homes for the homeless. This can result in a constant sense of feeling unfulfilled because no one person can heal these ailments in the world.

Struggling to Live a "Normal" Life

Many Empaths struggle to live a "normal" life. Because of how pain has integrated itself into everyday life and into the conditioning of society, many Empaths find themselves resenting normal life on every level. Still, they may also find themselves longing to live one. This can create inner conflict for any Empath. On the one hand, leading a life numb to pain and filled with misery is unbearable. On the other hand, you may find yourself just wanting to fit in. It may feel like you have never fit in, and you may blame your inability to be "normal" for the reason why you feel as though you never fit in. This can result in you feeling the inner conflict.

As an Empath, going to a mundane job that you dislike filled with people who are plagued by negative energy can be nonsensical and depressing. You may find yourself struggling to assimilate into this standard life. You may even become physically, mentally, and emotionally sick from trying to live this lifestyle. For many, there seems to be no alternative. This is why a growing majority of Empaths are choosing the entrepreneur path. Not only does it provide freedom from these soul-sucking experiences, but it also gives the Empath an opportunity to do something that truly has meaning for them.

The feeling of struggle does not end with a career, either. Many Empaths struggle to perform everyday activities such as going shopping, spending an extended amount of time with friends or family, or even watching certain things on TV or scrolling through social media. Because of their heightened sensitivities, this can be truly draining and overwhelming for an Empath.

Difficulty with Routines
Empaths and routines are typically not something that mixes well. Empaths tend to find themselves

struggling to deal with routines. As you may recall, Empaths feel things deeply and intensely. Often, this leads to an Empath always looking to have some sense of feeling that creates a deep sense of fulfillment.

You may find that you struggle to create a routine in your life and that staying aligned with a routine for any length of time is virtually impossible. You crave spontaneity, mystery, and change. In there, you find feelings that you love to explore and enjoy. This results in you feeling fulfilled and alive. For you, the routine may create numbness and a lack of emotional fulfillment. Finding ways to be spontaneous is a great way to ensure that you live your best life.

Weak Boundaries

Empaths are known to have weak boundaries, especially early in their development. Your ability to feel people deeply results in you regularly giving people the benefit of the doubt, often stepping into a dangerous cycle of allowing them to take advantage of you over and over again. This can be traumatic for Empaths who do not realize that they cannot save someone who has no desire to help themselves. You may have even been conditioned to abandon your boundaries from a young age, further weakening your boundaries. If this is the case, then you may already be aware of the symptoms you experience in your life as a result of weak boundaries.

Weak boundaries can also occur from a low sense of self-worth and self-esteem, which is common in Empaths. When you do not value yourself highly as an individual, you are more likely to tolerate toxic people and toxic environments. Having strong boundaries is all about saying "No!" more often and have no tolerance for anyone treating you wrongfully. Remove yourself from people and environments that do not have a positive impact on your life. As you work to increase your sense of self-worth and self-esteem and respect yourself more, you will naturally develop stronger boundaries.

The tendency to Have Addictions

If you are not adequately supported in your empathic gifts, you may feel drawn toward having addictions to support you in numbing out the pain and "trying to fit in." Many Empaths are reported to have "addictive personalities" because of this. It is important to understand that this behavior in an Empath is often rooted in a desire to relieve themselves of the pain that comes from feeling other's pain so deeply. This can add to the complexity of the addictions, meaning it is important to seek professional assistance in relieving these addictions should you find yourself facing them. Finding professional support that understands Empaths can be extra helpful, although it may be more challenging to find. When trying to remove the addiction, I would recommend replacing the particular addiction with something else in your life that is going to have a positive impact on your life. This could range from training at the gym, playing a team sport, learning how to dance, learning how to play a musical instrument, or starting your own business.

CHAPTER 4:

Understanding and Controlling Your Emotions

Emotions are one of the driving forces in everyone's life. We all have them, and they have seen us through many things, no matter who we are or how old we are. They were there when we went through devastating and painful heartbreaks, when we faced and survived some of our biggest fears, and when we needed the warning to move away from toxic situations. Of course, they aren't only there during the bad times.

They've given us the ability to feel the joys of true friendship, compassion for one another, and one of the strongest emotions of them all, to love as deeply as we can.

It's easy to let emotions lead the way, especially when one considers how strong and powerful they can be, but these feelings should always be met with reason and logic. That seems a tough one to think about, doesn't it? Emotional control is something not often heard of.

That being said, emotional control is a term I've heard a lot throughout my life. My mother, in particular, was the one who taught me about EQ. As an empath, it was something I often lost sight of by becoming too emotionally invested and/or involved. As a result, I often let my emotions rule me when I should have been ruling them. So, what exactly is EQ?

We all know what IQ is, right? Well, EQ is basically the emotional equivalent, being our emotional intelligence. Identifying and strengthening our EQ helps to enable us to control our emotions. It's the ability to recognize not only our own emotions but the emotions of others. We know empaths are especially good at feeling the emotions of others, but they aren't always good at telling the difference between these feelings and appropriately naming them, along with separating their own emotions from the emotions of others. That's why it's important to develop and understand EQ because you can use these feelings and emotions as a guide to manage and/or adjust emotions. Once you've learned to manage them, you'll be better equipped to adapt to environments, achieve your goals, and behave/think more appropriately in any given situation.

Having a good level of control over your emotions doesn't mean that you can't fall head over heels in love or that you can't have a bit of a mental breakdown every now and then. We are all human, after all. These are totally normal experiences to go through. That being said, there are certain emotions, such as jealousy and anger, that cause us to lose a fair bit of logic and reasonable thinking. This is where learning how to handle those negative emotions comes into play. If we don't handle them correctly, they could spiral out of control and pull us further down into a pit of negativity.

So, how do we become emotionally stronger and avoid disaster? I'm going to go through a few techniques on how to do exactly that below. These methods will also help make you more mentally stronger than ever before.

Use Your Body Language

Body language is the expressive nonverbal form of communication through body movements, facial expressions, and gestures. In general, our body language is a sequence of subconscious actions that portray our internal reaction to different situations. As with actual language, the way we move can show others how we feel and what we are thinking, just as we can learn what others are feeling and thinking based on the way they move.

How you communicate through movement and gestures is important. It can sometimes give away your true thoughts and emotions more honestly than a verbal reaction can because we often don't even mean to react in certain ways. The movement of the body is natural. The gestures we make don't need to be thought about. The way we raise our eyebrows is not something we consider doing beforehand.

Understanding body language is what makes it easier for us to pick up on how others react and feel toward us. Have you ever experienced someone constantly looking away or being easily distracted during a conversation? They just don't seem very interested in what you have to say, do they? Are there other times you can keep eye contact so long during an engaging conversation that you forget to blink? There is no "correct" way to use body language, but by being more fluid and relaxed with yourself and your body's movements, you can portray more positive reactions and can even make yourself more approachable. Take posture as another example; if you're uncomfortable in a social situation, you're more likely to tense up. To appear more comfortable, you can keep your head up straight while relaxing your shoulders. These simple gestures can give off the appearance that you are more at ease, even if you are experiencing stress at that point in time.

Being aware of your own movements and gestures is a good way to try to keep your emotions hidden and under control. Of course, it's not good to keep things bottled up, but as an empath, you don't want your heavy burden of feelings and emotions to flow out in certain situations. Stay strong and keep your head up. You know as well as I do that these negative emotions are fleeting. If you don't let them get to you and don't let others know that they're getting to you, you'll find that they are easier to release at the end of the day.

Use Positive Thinking

With so much negative energy in the world, it is often difficult to practice positive thinking.

Positive thinking starts with self-talk. Self-talk is easy enough to identify. It's the voice in all of our minds and the constant chain of thoughts that the voice repeats on a daily basis. Unfortunately, these thoughts are vulnerable to negativity and can lead you down the path of pessimism if you spend too long stuck inside your own head. This path is full of self-doubt and stress which, evidently, a sensitive empath—or anyone for that matter—does not need in their life. Therefore, we need to turn that voice into a positive one instead. Training yourself to have positive thoughts is better for your overall health; it can reduce stress levels and help you cope better in difficult situations. However; this mental training takes time because it always takes time to break any old habit.

Try appreciating and searching for humor during the day to lighten your mood. Be gentle and rational with yourself during the day by evaluating what you are really thinking and consider if it is positive or negative. Stop and take a deep breath whenever you catch those thoughts. Consider whether or not they are necessary or valid. If they aren't, turn them onto a new path. You may want to consider meditation as meditation is a fantastic way to train the mind to let go of thoughts, treating them like clouds that drift across the sky. You take note of these, but then you let them pass on by because you have no other choice. Surround yourself with positive and supportive people. It is much easier to forget and let go of bad thoughts when in the company of good friends who make you laugh more than anything else.

Remember that anything can have a positive twist to it if you try hard enough. After all, this can only benefit your emotional health. Positivity is not ignoring life's problems; it is taking these issues and turning them around to make the best of a bad situation.

You might drop the birthday cake at a big party, but simply because the beautiful icing was destroyed doesn't mean that it is inedible. It could be a story you look back at with a smile. It all depends on the way you react to the situation.

Use Positive Speaking

Words are one of the most powerful forces in the world, and they are conducted by one of the smallest organs of the human body. We don't always realize it, but what we speak out into the world does have an influence. Subconsciously, we follow what we hear. Think about what you're projecting out into the world; does it have a positive or negative impact on your life?

When you speak negatively, it only breeds more negative energy and can create fear and hopelessness. Sometimes it can worsen anxiety and other mental states such as depression and panic. Remember, your mental health is vastly important and relates directly to your emotional health.

People perceive you not only by the way you speak but also how you speak of yourself and others. We've all been in situations where we've either been gossiped about or criticized too harshly. These situations can easily be ignored, but most of the time, they do hurt us.

Whilst these terrible words and judgments can impact us enormously; positive speaking has just as much power. Through it, we can show love, our consideration for one another, and create reassurance where it is most needed.

Words are also a way to express your emotional overload, and simply talking about how you feel can be one of the biggest stress relievers. That being said, you need to be aware that it is unhealthy to complain all the time. As with positive thinking, you have the choice of how to look at your life. If you are constantly complaining, people will see you as a person who constantly complains. However, if you try to say something good every time you speak to someone, they'll remember that about you and so will you.

Evaluate your speech in the future and remember that positive speaking can definitely influence your emotions. Change your tone of voice if necessary. Let others know how you feel and use your words to embody who you are. If you want to be a positive person, it's up to you to make that happen. And if you want to release the negativity holding you back, you can do so with practice.

Create Your Own Personal Space

Is there a certain space you love, a place you can go where you can ponder over all your thoughts and feelings and feel safe and secure? It may be curled up in bed, or a spot in your favorite coffee shop, or a quiet corner of your local library. There are many possibilities. When we mention or talk about our own personal space, that's the type of image that comes to mind. That place of comfort and relaxation that belongs to you and only you, the one you might have thought of first, is your space. However, in this case, such a space is much more complex than a mere adored location.

Your own personal space is one that you set the boundaries for. You get to decide what goes and what doesn't. We set boundaries in place to protect ourselves both physically and emotionally. It's our own comfort zone where we can keep things at a distance, whether it's during physical or emotional interaction. Within this space, the act of overstepping a boundary can be anything that makes you uncomfortable in any way, be it someone being too loud around you when you don't like loud noise, someone sitting too close to you, or even a partner or friend wanting you to reveal something personal that you aren't willing to share. It's important to set these boundaries and stick to them. Any issues regarding them should be treated with care and seriousness, rather than being shrugged off.

When your personal space is compromised, you might feel drained, agitated, or upset with yourself for being angry and/or hurt. You might not even know the reason why you're reacting this way, especially if you haven't identified what your boundaries are. Your self-esteem might come crashing down due to this simple fact, which can hurt your confidence.

Overstepping boundaries is a form of violation. Some cases may be more intense compared to others, but they remain the same no matter how big or small your boundaries. It is important to define them for yourself.

We all have different needs and ideas of personal space. It is important to remember that it is okay to want your own. It is indeed personal, and it's perfectly all right to want that. Never feel bad for maybe needing more space than others. The important thing is that you acknowledge that you need it. We all do at times. Be clear, firm, and polite when explaining what your personal space is to people. Hopefully, they will respect you enough to accept them. In any circumstance where this does not happen, it is probably better to move on from the person and the situation. Your beautiful self does not deserve to be disrespected in that way.

That respect starts first with yourself. Respect yourself enough not to give in to pressure. It takes a lot of self-respect not to allow others to disrespect us.

Work on Time Management

Time management is crucial in our fast-paced lives. If we don't work on properly managing our time, we affect our emotions in adverse ways. An example of that includes that we stress and over-work ourselves, which can cause a storm of negativity. We're trying our best to avoid that negativity.

Now, some of us work best under pressure—which, to be honest, is not the best option—while others are more likely to start with their workload long in advance. Whichever way you choose to work, we are all prone to burn out. If we don't properly take care of ourselves, our time, and the amount of work we burden ourselves with, we can suffer from this.

Believe me; burnout isn't fun. If you've never experienced it, be thankful, and do your best never to reach that point. If you have, you'll know that you never want to experience it ever again.

Time management really is essential if you think about it. Our lives can't properly function without it. We would be late to appointments, overdue on work, and behind on bills to say the very least. So how are we supposed to manage it correctly?

Keep your thoughts clear and focus on the job at hand. Don't procrastinate. Where possible, avoid stress. That all sounds easy enough, doesn't it?

Now, of course, if we could all avoid stress, we would. Stress usually causes our bodies and our minds to grow tired quickly, making everything seem a little heavier than usual. If our body is a wreck, our mind will feel the same way, and so too will our emotions. Above all else, it's best to take breaks. We all need a break sometimes. This doesn't mean that you should work yourself to a breaking point and then take time off. No, you need short breaks in between too. These can be a simple, regular break while working to help with those short spans of concentration. Make a cup of tea, close your eyes for five minutes, and maybe practice some breathing exercises.

In the end, it really is about finding what works best for you. Good time management is an ongoing and constant practice. Try to prioritize in advance to save yourself all the emotional drainage and stress. You can even work on these during those short breaks. If you work them into your everyday schedule, you might feel the stress you experience at the idea of a break, start to slip away. It's all about working work and luxury into your schedule. Our bodies desperately require relaxation. Dedicating time to our mental and physical help can prevent burn out.

CHAPTER 5:

Raising Empathetic Children

An empathic child will have a nervous system that reacts strongly and quickly to external stimulus like stress.

Empathic children feel so much, and they don't understand how to manage this sensory overload. They experience more emotions. They have more intuition. They smell, hear, and see more. You might realize they don't like certain smells when you are cooking them dinner. A new perfume might make them sick. They may get headaches in harsh lighting or around loud talking. They like soft clothing, nature, beauty, and having just a few close friends.

Their senses get bombarded by the coarseness of the world, and this causes changes to their behavior. Most empathic children don't understand why they get upset. Parents that understand them can help find their triggers and give them solutions to help relieve their stress.

As parents, we need to understand what gets our empathic children over stimulated and stay away from these activities. Doing things that keep them calm will help with anxiety, tantrums, and exhaustion. Normal triggers might include: nightly news, violent movies or television shows, no alone time, multitasking, no breaks during the day, and too much running in one day. After being exposed to these factors, it might be harder for them to fall asleep. They may need more downtime to unwind before bed. It takes sensitive children longer to calm down because of the way their systems transition, which is at a slower pace than normal children. Empathic children absorb and feel other's emotional discomfort, especially from their close friends and parents. These children are "super-responders," which mean their hurts go deeper, and their joys are super joyous.

Empathic children don't have the filters to screen out chaos from crowds, noise, and light. Booing, clapping, and cheering can feel painful for them. They don't respond well to power tools, hammering, honking, or loud music. These sounds bother them when compared to the peaceful sound of wind chimes, water running, or birds chirping. Empathic children might cry more and try to deal with their feelings by finding places to be by themselves to try and handle their overloaded senses.

Most schools and society don't try to understand these exceptional children. Normal teachers and physicians will label them as fussy, antisocial, or shy. They get diagnosed with depression, anxiety disorder, or social phobia. They tend to be gentle, deep, thoughtful, and quieter instead of being assertive and very verbal. Because they have been wrongly diagnosed, your role as a parent is to support their wisdom, creativity, intuition, and sensitivity. We have to teach them a way to cope with their feelings.

Most empathic children don't get support from the parents, teachers, or physicians. It isn't because they aren't loved; it's because people don't understand what an empath is and don't know how to handle their needs. People don't know how to encourage their sensitivities. People will label them as too sensitive and tell them they need to get a thicker skin. Those types of comments will cause them to think something is wrong with them. They will feel invisible and misunderstood.

Understanding your empathic child is the first thing you have to do to help them bring out their best. You can support their sensitivities as a part of their depth, compassion, and excellence. Here are ways to tell if your child is an empath:

- Do they feel things deeply?

- Do they get overstimulated by stress, noise, crowds, or people?

- Do they strongly react to scary scenes and sad movies or books?

- Do they want to hide at family gatherings?

- Do they feel different than other children or think they don't fit in?

- Are they compassionate and good listeners?

- Do they surprise you with instinctive comments about others?

- Do they have strong connections to stuffed animals, animals, plants, or nature?

- Do they require more alone time?

- Do they take on their friend's sadness or stress?

- Do they take on your or other people's stress or emotions and act out when they get depressed, upset, or angry?

- Do they have just one friend or a few friends instead of a large network of friends?

To score this assessment:

If you answered yes to 9 to 12 questions, your child has very strong empathic traits.

If you answered yes to six to nine questions, your child has strong empathic traits.

If you answered yes to four to eight questions, your child has moderate empathic traits.

If you answered yes to one to three questions, your

child has some empathic traits.

If you answered no to all of the questions, your child has absolutely no empathic traits.

Children who are empath are precious beings. It doesn't matter where your child lands on the spectrum; they would benefit from you teaching them about their sensitivities.

CHAPTER 6:

Empathy in Your Relationships

Everybody wants to find a soul mate, have a close friend, and connect with their family. However, empathic people struggle in this area for unique reasons. Romance is especially hard for the empath.

The empathic person tends to have a pretty hard time when it comes to finding romantic relationships. It's interesting when you know two empaths that have both have mental scars get together, and then they have a really hard time getting past feeling each other's hidden issues and pains.

They could spend hours arguing with each other about how they know something is wrong with them, only to have the other say they knew their partner was upset with them.

The real problem is this.
Empaths can scare the crap out of you.

It can be exciting, especially if you are an empath, to meet another empath that could be a romantic partner. You would think that they would express their feelings faster than non-empaths. And they do because they know their feelings, unlike others who second guess. That means, it could just be weeks into your relationship, and they could say, "I love you." Nothing can change the empathic person's mind about how they feel, and this can end up ruining relationships, sometimes.

The empath can get moody.
This is tough for romantic relationships as well as friendships. Because of their strong emotions, things can sometimes get out of control. Many times, the feelings that are coursing through an empaths body won't even be their own. The problem is they could have absorbed too much energy from their loved one. This could end up being targeted back to the owner of the emotion. It's unfair that the empath gets blamed, but it's how it tends to work out.

Inconsistency could create more struggles.

Empaths do not like it when what a person says does not match what they do, or what they feel since an empath can pick up on all this stuff. It's tough on them when they have to call bullshit on their friends, family, and partners. This becomes extremely rough when they are living in close quarters with their loved one. An empath can pick up on every little smudge on the surface of honesty.

Empaths are able to pick up on complacency.

You know how some relationships can reach a plateau, well; empaths are able to sense that quickly. All new relationships will reach a point where things taper off and settle. It's not necessarily a bad thing; it just means it has leveled out. Empaths will notice this and can end up panicking. They may end turn to stirring up trouble to get some intensity back in the relationship. Their partner that can't detect this will find the empath strange when it's really just a gift that has gone awry.

Empaths can't give up.

Empaths won't divorce, break up, or dissolved romantic relationships, really any relationship, even if this may be the best option. Empathic people will always be able to see potential in the other person because they feel the frustration in the relationship.

The struggle happens when an empath is married to a person who isn't in touch with their feelings, and divorce comes up. The empath will want to try to hold things together with no matter what. Imagine that there is a person who is more compatible with the empath, but they won't know that because they will continue to try to revive what's lost.

Empaths like their own space, but don't like being alone.

A lovely conundrum, isn't it? While it may seem strange, if you analyze it correctly, it makes sense. Empaths love being in love and love to spend time with their romantic partner, but when they are in need of their space, they have to get it. They become more emotional when they can't partake in their personal time. They have to have time to recuperate and energize themselves.

They don't get taken seriously.
This is the biggest problem for any relationship an empath may have, romantic or not. They will have ideas that could seem far-fetched, but if given the benefit of the doubt and space, they will show just how much their own words mean. This tends to be a struggle for most relationships because many people will say things and only do them 40% of the time.

People are used to only believing less than half of what others say, especially in close relationships. The thing is an empath will say they can do something, and they really are able to do it, and they will do it. That's why it hurts so much when others don't believe them.

It's important that the empathic family members, friends, and romantic partners are taken seriously. Empaths are the most real people out there, and that's why they tend to struggle in relationships.

Relationship Sabotage

As you have probably already figured out, empaths are prone to experiencing more relationship problems than a non-empath. They also respond to these problems in very different and unusual ways, which are not always healthy. The following are various ways that an empath may sabotage their relationships:

1. They compromise boundaries without being asked to.

An empath will often feel their partner's needs in such a profound way that they decide to give into them in ways that end up hurting them. They could choose to negate a boundary that their partner wouldn't ask them to cross. When they make this decision without letting their partner know, the empath will open themselves to resentment and anger. Their partner will end up not understanding what happened. They become confused and frustrated because of it.

2. They will quit expressing their own needs.

An empath can become so focused on making their

partner happy that they end up neglecting themselves. An empath is extremely prone to forgetting how important it is for them to express their needs and making sure that they get met. This will end up causing things to happen that are similar to the first point. The empath will start to feel neglected, and their partner won't understand.

3. The neglect self-care.

Again, because they are so concerned about others emotional wellbeing, they will neglect themselves. When they get too focused on somebody else, they can sometimes neglect the things that make them who they are. This could mean that they spend less time with their friends, less energy for things they like to do, and less focus on their work that they find meaningful. This will damage their esteem and happiness.

4. They will end up creating a parent-child relationship.

By nature, empaths are nurturers. They will often try

to meet the needs of their partner before their partner has expressed them. This can become a dangerous dynamic because it becomes a one-sided relationship. The empath will end up becoming resentful of their obligations. The partner will also become resentful because they will lose their autonomy.

5. Important problems will be solved in their head.

It's very common for an empath in keeping a running dialogue in their head, and they will take on both sides of the argument. The empath will often resolve the issue in their head, and they won't even bring the issue to light. This could get rid of the problem, but it can end up creating a new one. It's unfair to the partner, who is probably not even aware that conflict has happened. It robs them of autonomy, their chance to defend themselves, and the opportunity to understand the empaths viewpoint.

Make sure that if you are an empath that you don't become prey to your own devices. Try to find these behaviors and fight against them so that you can create healthy relationships.

CHAPTER 7:

How Empaths Can Understand and Help Other People

I've already mentioned this, but I want to give you a deeper insight into how empaths can help people. We've already established that they're drawn to healing and bear the type of personality that wants the world to be a better place, but how do they go about making it one? Sure, compassion is a huge part of empathy, but what else can they do? I'd be happy to tell you.

The good that an empath wishes to do—or, rather, is capable of doing—is quite dependent on what type of empath they are. Naturally, pardon the pun, the environmental/geomantic empath has more of a pull to fix the earth. This is the same for the plant/flora empath. When an empath homes their gifts, they can use them to maintain balance and restore harmony into the world. They have their own unique ways of doing this.

Empaths are fantastic listeners. They genuinely care about and enjoy learning about others, mostly because they can feel the emotions of the other person. There's a sort of rush you feel when someone tells you their stories as it can feel as though you were actually there. When someone needs support, an empath can perceive that and provide it accordingly. The empath can sense things like fear or danger, and if they've strengthened their gifts or are attuned to them, they can use the skills and adaptations they've developed to remove themselves and others from such a situation. They don't talk about themselves much, but if they do, it reveals that they have a great deal of trust in the person they're sharing with. Often, however, people seem to trust them quickly. This is because they relate to others in their own unique way.

It is because of this relatability that people feel a pull toward empaths. It doesn't matter if the empath is aware of their empathic abilities; people will still be drawn to them. People are willing to pour their hearts and souls out to empaths who are complete strangers without necessarily intending to do so. It happens on a subconscious level.

Needless to say, sometimes the empath needs that release too. That's why it's imperative that they find some of their own kind or they keep those special friends close. They're exceptional people.

Another way empaths use their abilities to bring good into the world is the ability to solve problems. Since they enjoy learning as much as they do, they study many things, and this means they are constantly sharpening their minds. Sometimes this is a subconscious action. The empath brings new meaning to the saying: "Where there is a will, there is a way."

Though it helps others, you should be wary of the fact that people will often want to offload their problems onto you. These people might not even know you. If you don't keep your guard up and strengthen your energy, these problems can convert into being your problems. Make sure that you keep the two separate. You don't want to be dragged on. Be honest with yourself and others. If a situation feels like it is going to bring negativity your way, it is okay to take a step back and tell the other person that you can't handle it. This is an act of self-preservation.

I know that sometimes it might feel like you are thrown into scenarios aimlessly, and in them, you drink up the emotions of others, but you are stronger than you think. Empaths have to be strong to be able to carry both their own feelings and the feelings of others. Consider yourself a type of energy warrior. You absorb all this energy and transform it into something valuable. You have the ability to shift the negative to positive. Purify the world. If anyone can do it, an empath can.

Remember how I said compassion is one of the best ways for an empath to avoid emotional distress? Some empaths find that they need to be in a constant state of compassion in order not to suffer adverse effects from outside influences. Others try to be as open as they can be, allowing each feeling and sensation to pass through without much notice, and in doing so, they release all judgment and try to be as honest and carefree as possible. Then there are the empaths who believe in crystal healing in order to transfer and create energetic healing. The empath who heals the world in whatever manner they need to is the empath who has a great sense of inner peace and balance because they know that they are following their calling in life.

If you've already found what you're meant to be doing—say, for instance, mine is releasing my creativity into the world in any manner I deem appropriate—then you know what I mean by feeling a sense of balance. If you're still looking, don't give up. Follow your intuition, and it won't lead you astray.
Bear in mind that you may fail a few times. You may think that you've found that thing you're meant to be doing only to realize that it was nothing more than a step toward where you're meant to be. Keep searching even when you hit this wall. You are on the journey you are following for a reason. That reason will reveal itself to you soon. An empath's gut is usually right.

CHAPTER 8:

Energy Vampires and Psychic Attacks

Energy vampires are the people around you that drain your life force. Spending some time with an energy vampire will leave you feeling sapped, shattered, and unhappy. Energy vampires are such a negative force in society; we should do our best to understand both their nature and impact and safeguard ourselves against their malicious intent.

Different types of energy vampires.

- Dominating vampire

This type of vampire is a master at the power play. They love to feel superior. And they also love to exercise their power (real or imagined) over their targets. Most of the times, their desire to control people stems from the emotional trauma they underwent in their early childhood. They may or may not remember those traumatic incidents. Generally, the dominating vampire tends to want to control the concepts and thoughts of their target. Also, they tend to have strong opinions, and their stand is unshakable. A dominating vampire can only feel good about themselves when they succeed in making a target submissive.

- The hypercritical vampire

Nobody is ever safe when it comes to this vampire. They can spot you from a long way off and immediately find fault. The judgmental empath may be seen as being hard on other people, but the truth is that they are unconsciously harsh on themselves too. It usually stems from a lifetime of trying to win someone's approval and yet failing, and the weight of failure pushes them into becoming hateful.

Judgmental vampires are especially fond of targets that appear to have low self-esteem. They are masters at the art of deception and gaslighting, and they could easily make you hate yourself.

- The overdramatic vampire

These vampires are a special breed. They come into

your life with the aim of creating drama and then having you tied into their drama as you take on the role of "savior." The overdramatic empire is created out of an emptiness that they have battled since their childhood. This vampire can also be created out of a need to reclaim lost glory. For instance, if someone was famous in high school and college, but upon finishing school, they realized that they were powerless roosters, they may turn into overdramatic vampires. These people are too cunning, and they just know the perfect angle to strike so as to make the curtains roll.

- Narcissistic vampire

This type of energy vampire is very common. They are egocentric parasites with no ounce of empathy.
Narcissists are only concerned about what you can do for them, about what you can give them, and once the supply is over, they discard you and go hunting for a new target. The perfect opportunity for a narcissist to bring out their true colors is in relationships. Initially, the narcissist, a master of charm, tries to make

themselves appear as heaven-sent angels, but once the relationship starts gathering momentum, their viciousness slowly starts coming out.

- Victim vampire

This type of vampire tries to get others to feel guilty. If you have ever interacted with a victim vampire, you are at risk of becoming their next villain. Victim vampires commonly paint the world as a dark place filled with evil people who are out to use you and toss you on the side of the road. The average victim vampire will have numerous spins to an invented story, and they will conveniently mention their targets so as to gain people's sympathy. This disorder is usually triggered by being abandoned and mistreated in their early childhood.

Energy vampires put empaths through a lot of pain, so it is upon the empath to figure out a way to ward off energy vampires. If left to do as they wish, the energy vampire would ultimately ruin an empath.

The Reasons Behind Vampirism & Narcissism

These people feel cut off from themselves and deep down feel unworthy of being loved, which stops them from getting their own needs met. The only way they can get what they need is to take it from others. Due to their unconnectedness to themselves, they are unable to find fulfillment within, so this void is then filled by stealing energy from other people. They prey on easy targets, i.e., those with weak boundaries which can easily be drained.

Energy vampires are often singled out for being evil and harmful, but their actions are often unconscious. They don't know what they are doing. They are victims themselves, although this doesn't make it any easier on us. The paradox is that the energy vampire and the victim are similar on some level. They have been drawn together, and that is why the vampire is able to attach to the victim through this identification. The opposites have attracted one another.

Narcissists are often attracted to empaths and people in healing or spiritual circles as these people are the most open and loving. This makes them easy prey for an energy vampire. They will usually stay attached to these people for a long time, due to the victim's non-resistance. On the surface, it will probably look like a positive friendship.

It is also worth mentioning that while certain people are energy vampires per se, most people have some vampirism tendencies depending upon their mood. If someone you know, a friend perhaps, is going through a particularly tough time they may unconsciously reach out in an energy-sucking way, as they seek an uplift in their mood. They probably won't realize they are doing this, but empaths should be on their guard against it. Telephone calls are one of the main ways friends can steal your energy. If a friend calls you regularly to talk about their problems, you may want to withdraw and detach consciously from the conversation emotionally. Be there to listen but not to take on their negative energy. Over time your friend will probably recognize they do not get a boost from unloading their problems onto you, so will probably stop sharing their personal issues as much. This doesn't mean your friendship with them will end, but you are just setting a boundary between what is yours and what is theirs. Remember that a healthy relationship are based on balance and an equal amount of giving and taking.

How to deal with energy vampires.

01. Stop broadcasting your life

One of the greatest challenges of modern technology is that it has enabled us to lead pretty loudly. In a perfect world, everyone would live as they wanted to and no one would bother them, but then we live in a flawed world, where people will make your life their business. When you broadcast your life through Social Media, the energy vampire is watching. You give them ideas on how they may attack you, especially the judgmental vampire, and the narcissistic vampire, both of whom would like to tear you down. Avoid yapping about your secrets, plans, and opinions to every person you encounter, and it will give energy vampires less material to work with.

02. Become a master at recognizing the threat

Some energy vampires have finessed their craft. They don't just show up and start sapping the life force out of you. It is usually a slow, irreversible attack, staged in such a manner you won't think them, perpetrators. Energy vampires can be very pretentious. When you realize that someone consistently makes you exhausted, nauseated, and irritated, you should recognize them for the energy vampire that they are and put some distance between yourself and that person. Apart from noticing their negative impact, you should also try to establish their end goal. More often than not, an energy vampire will have a hidden motive besides draining people of their life force, and this agenda of theirs will almost always have a sadistic tone.

03. Schedule your time

The people who commonly fall prey to energy

vampires are those without a sense of direction in their lives. When you don't have a plan on how to use your time, what happens is that you are much more likely to engage in time-wasting activities, giving the energy vampire an opportunity to zero in on you. But if you move according to your schedule, you will have less time for non-productive meetings, thus discouraging the scheming energy vampire. Also, when you have a schedule, you are much more likely to practice mindfulness, i.e., living the moment fully, and this will help you pick up on the energy vampire's agenda quite early on.

04. Avoid arguments

Nothing gets an energy vampire more animated than an argument. They are happy about finding someone to roll in the mud with. This is their perfect time to sap your energy, plant wild ideas into your mind, and bring confusion into your day, and possibly life.
Knowing that an energy vampire will always be looking for an opportunity to engage in arguments, you should deny them that chance by making yourself

scarce. Their strategies are subtle, relentless, knowing too well that at some point, you will give up, but you must stay true to your word. Stay away from arguments.

05. Meditate

This exercise helps in clearing away the negative energy in your mind planted by energy vampires. The energy vampire can attack you suddenly, or they can skillfully send small pockets of negative energy, and as time passes, you fall into their very well thought out the trap. If you fail to rid yourself of their negative energy, chances are they'll ultimately outsmart you. Meditation helps you get rid of this negative energy, which means it helps you gain clarity into what's happening both around and within you. Meditation fortifies your spiritual body, making it hard for an energy vampire to take advantage of you.

06. Make their disrespect costly

Most energy vampires are driven into action by forces such as pride, jealousy, ego, hatred, and personal beliefs. Some energy vampires are subtle in their attacks while others are openly hostile, especially the judgmental vampire. Commonly, empaths tend to ignore or play down instances where energy vampires disrespect them. They should lose the cowardice and turn the tables on energy vampires. It doesn't matter what role an energy vampire plays; the victim can still get their justice. For instance, they can campaign to the public over the matter, attracting public sympathy and an outcry. Or they may report the offender to government institutions and punitive measures would be taken. When an energy vampire realizes that some people cannot be taken advantage of, it humbles them.

07. Consume healthy meals

The brain relies on the energy generated from what we eat. If we consume bland diets, our bodies will have low energy levels and limit the brain's activities. The brain is a major defense organ when it comes to warding off energy vampires. The healthier you are, the brighter the light shields you can form around you. So, ensure that you are consuming a diet rich in vitamins, minerals, and other essential compounds. Studies also show that there's a direct link between what we consume and our mental health. People who are used to poor diets are at risk of developing mental disorders, whereas those who eat rich diets tend to have powerful brains. When you have a healthy brain, it becomes far easier to block energy vampires from sapping your energy.

CHAPTER 9:

Cleansing Negative Energies

Good hygiene is recognized as an excellent way to maintain health and prevent disease. The same principle that applies to hand washing holds true for subtle energetic cleansing as well. When the system is functioning well, energy is used efficiently, and there is neither a deficit nor excess. The vast majority of people are operating on a fraction of the energy available to the human system.

Proper focus and discipline are necessary in order to tap into — and efficiently use — these energy reserves. One of the steps in doing so is making sure you are not being bogged down with excess energy. This is something that tends to happen to empaths, and the accumulation sparks a myriad of issues. Anxiety, panic attacks, depression, lethargy, and other health problems are all possible if extra, negative energy is not cleansed from the system.

Thankfully, there are multiple ways to clear your aura. If you're feeling heavy, burdened, or if being bombarded by external sources has been a problem, it is a good idea to clear on a weekly or even daily basis. In time, it will be easier to know when clearing is necessary. A simple method is through prayer or the use of a mantra. Many faiths have specific prayers or figures to call upon for protection, and this is an excellent way to accomplish your goal.

If this is not familiar, you can create a simple prayer asking that negative energy be removed from the system. Sacred sounds or "mantras" are recited to invoke what is being called upon. A Sanskrit mantra for protection of the body from oncoming danger is: "Om Hreem Hreem Hreem Hreem Hreem Hum Fatt." Chant this whenever you sense danger is coming towards you.

Smudging is another wonderful tool that has been around for ages. This is the burning of specific dried plants or resins whose smoke cleanses and drives away negative energy. Sage is the most well-known, but there are many different smudges, including cedar, sweetgrass, lavender, mugwort, juniper, pinon, copal, frankincense, and myrrh. They have different properties and can be combined for specific purposes. For example, sage is very good at cleansing, while sweetgrass is known to welcome positive energies.

Burning them together can be especially good. Smudge is either tied into a bundle called a "smudge stick" or comes loose and is burned in a fireproof vessel. Smudging is simple. Just light the smudge, blow out the flame, and pass or fan the smoke over the whole body. After the individual is smudged, smudge the room, home, or area as well — to remove any lurking, stagnant energy. This is another good practice to do regularly.

A bath with sea salt or sage clears the aura in a similar fashion. Sage baths have traditionally been used for sore and aching muscles, but are also beneficial for cleansing. To prepare a sage bath, do the following:

1. Take three ounces/100 grams of dried rubbing

sage and put it in cheesecloth, a cotton pillowcase, or a knee-high stocking.

2. Tie off the end and place it into a bathtub full of hot water, like a tea bag. Let the bag of sage become wet, wring it out, and repeat a few times.

3. Remove the bag and soak in the waters for twenty minutes or more. The bag can be dried and reused up to three times.

Gemstones can act as an alternative, as they are also capable of cleansing negative energy. Fluorite is especially beneficial for removing bad energy from the aura, while amethyst and quartz balance and protect it. Placing a piece of selenite in each corner of the home after smudging can also be beneficial, as this creates a protective forcefield.

Amulets like a cross, yantra, or medicine wheel can be worn to ward off negative vibrations. Other tools like the mezuzah and hamsa hand can be used in the home to help maintain a positive, energetic level.

Arts like feng shui are specifically designed to create harmony in one's living space. Empaths often feel like their home is their sanctuary and fortress against the world, but this can still be flooded by negative input. Deliberate arrangement and balance of the home optimizes how energy flows, and creates a rejuvenating place of rest.

If the negativity is triggering anxiety attacks, there are several simple, holistic steps you can take to help reverse the condition. They will be beneficial not only for panic attacks but for any of the other symptoms as well.

1. Get deep, long-lasting sleep.

Too many people neglect their sleep, especially now that technology provides 24/7 entertainment. Keep your cell phone and any other unnecessary technology out of the bedroom. Making good quality sleep a priority will work wonders for agitation. Having a set bedtime helps establish a rhythm that tells the body it's time to rest.

Avoiding overstimulation thirty minutes before hitting the sack is ideal and doing anything that helps one unwind, like reading, journaling, or meditating, sets the tone for a restful night. Scents like lavender promote relaxation and rest, as well as chamomile tea and natural sleep supplements like valerian root.

2. Eat well and exercise daily.

There are many, many diets and exercise programs out there, so keep it simple. Eat more fresh, wholesome foods with plenty of fruits and vegetables, and reduce or eliminate processed foods. Daily exercise can be as basic as starting the day with a ten-minute walk or stretching.

The more vigorous daily activity works wonders for some, and mind-body exercises like yoga and tai chi are especially helpful for empaths. Their movements are designed to balance and harmonize the body's energy on a subtle level, while also strengthening the physical body.

3. Do breathing exercises.

The breath becomes quick and ragged when under stress. The quality of the breath is a direct gauge of one's emotions and state of mind. Take some time to observe your breath and see how often it is unsteady. Simple breathing exercises will quickly calm the mind and help the body to relax and re-center.

The following practice focuses on making the inhales and exhales of the same duration:

α. Choose a count (four or six is good to start) and count to that number on the inhale.

β. Exhale to the same count.

χ. Do this for a few minutes, or until the anxiety passes.

4. Avoid caffeine and other stimulants.

Stimulants may help with focus in the short term, but make anxiety skyrocket in the long term. This includes coffee, tea, and, yes, even chocolate. Furthermore, stimulants are hard on the adrenal glands, the anatomy responsible for the fight-or-flight response and buffering stress. Good adrenal health is linked to the healthy root chakra. Try switching to decaf, herbal tea, or lemon water.

5. Mindfulness meditation.

The mind spends most of its time dwelling in the past or fretting over the future. Being mindful, or present in the now, is a panacea for the meandering and a cure for discontent. Mindfulness meditation can be performed when sitting quietly with crossed legs or in a straight-backed chair.

It really is as simple as it sounds:

a) As you are sitting, focus on the current setting.

b) Become aware of the sound of your breath, any other noises in the room, any smells or visuals.

c) Feel the cushion or chair under your body.

d) Any thoughts that arise in your mind are to be acknowledged and allowed to pass.

Doing this for ten or twenty minutes daily is recommended. It can also be done during any daily activities with the goal of being mindful in all tasks. When washing the dishes, for example, be present in action. Do it slowly and lovingly. Be aware of every second of the action.

Mindfulness improves focus and reduces anxiety. It also makes people proactive instead of reactive. If an empath is being hit by a wave of input, mindful meditation will make it easier to think on one's feet and do what needs to be done to solve the situation rather than panicking and making it worse.

If an anxiety attack hits, grounding is the first step to take. Empaths can potentially receive waves upon waves of anxiety, and anchoring the system protects against external input. If this is ineffective, try mentally saying, "No!" with intent. It doesn't matter if you know where the waves are coming from or not. Refusing to allow the exchange can stop it dead in its tracks. Bending over and letting the blood rush to the head will help with the spacey sensation, and tugging on the earlobes pacifies the system.

If you are at home or trying to sleep, wrapping blankets tightly around the body like a cocoon soothes and calms. Using any of the previously mentioned tools are an option, and sometimes all that is necessary is making contact with a close or loved one. If nothing is working, let the panic attack ends naturally. Acknowledge that it is only anxiety and cannot cause any serious damage. Say that it will pass in five to fifteen minutes if one refuses to panic.

Do anything to make yourself more comfortable and then wait. Remember that prevention is the best cure and experiment with ways to do away with the episodes.

Humans are a part of the natural world, but it is easy to forget this as we walk around in our concrete jungles. Experts warned the public at the turn of the century that big city-living is detrimental to health. Spending time in nature is one of the simplest and most effective ways to rebalance the system, ground, and rid the body of stagnant energy. It is especially important if you are currently residing in an urban area. Doing this regularly is a wonderful boost to health and happiness, and a potent preventative against falling ill.

Make spending time outdoors a regular part of your routine, and use this time as a source of pleasure. Bringing plants into your home and planting a garden are alternative or additional routes to take. Performing the aforementioned exercises in the wilderness can amplify their impact.

A more delicate matter is the healing of old emotional wounds. While the gifts of the empath are not pathological, many of the accompanying attitudes are. Poor boundaries, codependency, and being overly sensitive are signs of self-neglect. The empath who uses every technique available will only receive fleeting relief if old, underlying issues are not addressed.

They will be different depending on the person, and being brave enough to face these problems will be freeing in the long term. This kind of healing takes time and work and may require a variety of interventions. Alternative medicine, energy healing, and bodywork will realign your physical energies and assist with removing that which hurts. Psychotherapy is another option, and others find release in solitude, contemplation, and self-reflection.

The power of love should never be underestimated, and tender relationships can be highly transformational in nature. Devotion and surrender to the bigger picture can instantly heal the pain that no other efforts have been able to touch.

CHAPTER 10:

Setting Energetic Boundaries

Growing up in a relatively small town, I never truly understood just how sensitive I was until later in life (even though I was painfully shy in my youth). My sensitivity was all that I had known, and therefore, I thought it was normal. In the back of my mind, I always felt different from others, but I wasn't able to pinpoint why this was. When I reached my 30's however, I decided to move to a big city for a brand-new experience. As soon as I set foot into this new place, I noticed a huge difference from where I had grown up. I could feel an energetic difference in the atmosphere. It just felt different, and I really struggled to settle there. My body always felt on alert, and I found it increasingly difficult to relax. For the first six months, I even struggled to sleep, as the energy of the place was much faster paced, then what I had been used to. Also, due to the much higher volumes of people, I couldn't go anywhere where I wasn't surrounded by others. By the end of the day, I would feel completely worn out. Even though I would work to keep my own energy high, going out would eventually leave me feeling drained. This was because I hadn't learnt how to set energetic boundaries for myself, where I would be able to hold my own energy and stop others from infiltrating and intruding on my space. Evidentially, the people I would come into contact with day to day, would rob me of my high positive energy (which I had been working hard to maintain) and leave me with their low negative crappy energy. It is no real wonder I was worn out!

However, I learnt an awful lot from spending a year in a busy city; I finally understood myself to be an empath. Although I was tired most of the time, it enabled me to finally learn how to hold my energy better and shield myself from others. It was the only way an empath could survive in a heavily populated place. Many big cities are almost intrusive of personal space, especially on public transport. It is not energetically healthy for an empath or sensitive person to be in such close proximity to other people. They will easily pick up other energy in these environments unless they can learn to develop strong firm boundaries. If you are in public places often, then start to use these as practice in maintaining energetic boundaries. I would even suggest avoiding rush hours and extremely busy areas if possible until you have developed firm enough boundaries to be able to handle these places.

How To Set Boundaries

Empaths have the problem of not being able to feel their own needs deeply enough because they are so overwhelmed by the feelings and wants of others. This is why they need to develop even stronger boundaries than a non-empathic person.

Their boundaries are far too permeable to others when they should instead be much firmer in order to provide them with a strong, energetic foundation of support. Lacking adequate boundaries in our interactions with others, means we find it extremely difficult to say no, which can often lead to empaths being taken advantage of. One of the hardest things for an empath to understand (because of the way they are made to feel) is that it is not their job to make others happy. They must learn how to make themselves happy first.

The first step in creating healthier boundaries is by increasing your self-confidence. Most of us have been brought up and conditioned through society and by our caregivers that being agreeable means that we are well behaved and therefore good. With these types of beliefs, we often disown our own opinions, which result in a lack of confidence. This is a violation against our true selves, especially when we carry these types of beliefs into adulthood. Following the exercises in this book will help to improve your self-confidence, there are also countless sources available online for helping increase confidence.

The second step in setting a strong, energetic boundary is to be in non-resistance to the other people we are protecting ourselves from. This can be initially quite difficult, especially if others have been infiltrating our space for some time. But without releasing this resistance, we will be unable to prevent them from breaking our boundaries again. It is easy to judge people who are impeding on us. By having an emotional reaction to and judging the people we are trying to keep out, we actually make it easier for them to penetrate our boundary again, which weakens it even further.

The next key to developing boundaries is to have a strong sense of grounding. This is essentially connecting our body to the Earths energy. The whole energetic area (about an arm's length all around you) should be connected to the Earth, not just the area which we cover physically.

01. Oils and Incense

Plant oils and incense sticks have been used for ground for thousands of years. Herbs such as sage and cedar are still very popular to help cleanse a negative area while bringing positive energy into it. Sage, in particular, which gives off an incense-like scent, is often used to clear negativity. Essential oils can also be used for the same purpose.

02. Water

Water could be described as an empaths best friend. It can be used in numerous ways to help with grounding. Taking a quick shower or bath has an incredible effect as it removes and neutralizes the empaths energy. You can even go out in the rain, go swimming, or just go and sit next to the water. Adequate daily consumption of water is also highly recommended. Almost any use of water will have a positive grounding effect.

03. Walk barefoot

Probably the most common grounding technique out there and it's easy to do. Simply remove your shoes and walk on the Earth. It can be in your backyard, out in nature, on the beach, or anywhere you feel comfortable. By physically feeling the Earth beneath your feet allows you to feel connected while helping to rebalance your emotional state.

Breathing Techniques For Protection

1. Find a quiet, peaceful place. Get yourself into a centered and still mindset. Start by paying all of your attention onto your breath. Breathe in through your nose and out through your mouth.

2. When breathing out, imagine creating a bubble around you. However far you envision your breath going out, is what defines your own personal space. Usually, an arm's length radius is sufficient.

3. This bubble should encompass all around you; if there was someone close behind, you would easily detect their presence since your bubble is sensitive to their energy.

4. Your bubble has the ability to expand and contract. For example, you can consciously make it expand when you're public speaking or at a party, or whenever you need to be expressive or seen. On the other hand,

whenever you're are in a busy, overwhelming environment or do not want to be noticed, you can constrict your bubble and pull it in towards your body. This helps protect from being intruded upon by others.

5. During this process, you want to begin working with this bubble. As you breathe in, imagine this bubble pulling inward. But, when breathing outward, imagine the bubble expanding. Learn to control this boundary through visualization and through your breath consciously.

6. Working consciously with your breath is the most important factor in this exercise. Focus on your breath whenever you feel you need protection from others or from an overstimulating environment.

7. Always visualize your bubble as a strong boundary which protects you easily. See it as clear with no tears or holes in it.

8. If you feel someone has infiltrated your area with their emotions or energy, during the exhale phase, imagine pushing this unwanted energy out and away from your space. By becoming more conscious of your own space, you will easily become aware when this bubble is penetrated against your wish. This can often be through a feeling or emotion.

9. With practice, you will feel and become aware of the presence of this protective bubble. This will enable you to work with and control it much easier.

10. Everyone has an aura or energy space around them, but most people do not take responsibility for what they allow to enter this space. Therefore, they often pick up things which do not belong to them. This technique works to protect your own positive energy by preventing others from robbing it from you or exchanging it for their negativity.

There is no right or wrong way to do this; if it feels right to you, it will serve its intended purpose. Feel free to alter parts of this process if you believe it works better.

Practice these boundary techniques as often as possible or until it becomes habitual. Then eventually you will unconsciously control your bubble of protection without even thinking about it. Reaching this point requires some dedication to the practice.

Without learning how to draw energetic boundaries, our aura can become too expansive and project outward from us, up to many meters away. If for example, you have a garden full of animals, unless you build a fence around the garden, the animals will roam away, and you will likely lose most of them. In the same way, we need to build a metaphorical fence around us to contain our energy. If the aura projects too far outwards, let us say at a 5-meter radius all around, then we will pick up whatever is in that area. When out in public, that is potentially a lot of unwanted energy and things which can stick to us.

Without learning to control the aura through a firm boundary, some of our power and vital life energy is lost. But by making a conscious decision to reclaim your energy by pulling it in towards you significantly reduces any losses. The normal resting place for the aura or energy boundary should be close to the body, no more than an arms width radius. This boundary can be consciously expanded through breathwork and visualizing whenever you need to be seen or heard by others. Exercising to constrict and expand your boundary will strengthen your space and allow you more protection from others while also enabling you to be seen.

Healthy boundaries will also help empaths from losing their vital energy through cracks and leaks in the aura. This usually occurs in crowded public places, as our life force can be rapidly sucked away.

Tips For Setting Boundaries

Empath Meditation

Meditation should be the cornerstone of building a healthy and happier life for an empath. It works to reset the mind and body. Sensitives can meditate while imaging themselves engulfed in a white bubble of light, which is made of love and protection.

Envision this bubble as something which keeps all negativity out. Similar to the grounding technique above, meditate with the aim to keep yourself guarded from unwanted things. The benefits of meditation are incredible if you aren't meditating at the moment.

Here is another good reason to start.

Scan and Check

Another handy tip for sensitives is to scan their bodies through their attention and awareness before going out anywhere. By working to feel within your own body and checking for emotions or pains before going out, this will allow you to feel what is already there, in other words, what is yours. Then when out of the house, you should be able to detect any different emotions or energies which were not present earlier. This is something you likely picked up from someone else.

Mantra

This is a quick and powerful way to create protection if you don't have the time to meditate or ground yourself. It involves creating a mantra for protection but holding a firm belief in its effectiveness is key.

Create a mantra for yourself and memorize it so you can use it if and when you need it. An example, of a protection mantra, could be something like 'I am encompassed in the light of love and protection. I am protected against any and all negative energies and their effects. Nothing negative can harm or affect me'.

You can repeat this mantra in your head or silently to yourself if you feel particularly overwhelmed and feel the need for protection. Affirm this statement while keeping your intention within your body, scanning for any physical sensations. This will naturally strengthen your energy and aura.

Block or not?

A final word on boundaries, most empaths will eventually learn how to block all external energy coming their way. Although this is a healthy way to tackle the situation for newly learned sensitives, longer-term this may not be the best solution. By blocking all external energies, we are also blocking positive messages coming our way. To live creatively and fully, we need to recognize what is going on around us. When setting the intention of creating a solid boundary, it is beneficial to consciously decide to make it permeable to positive energy, only if you feel comfortable doing this. If you're new to set energetic boundaries, then it would be best to stick with blocking all energies and then with expertise and time, understand what you want to let in and what you do not.

CHAPTER 11:

Overcoming Your Fears, Grasping Your Power, And Nurturing Your Empathic Abilities

Hopefully, as you read the introduction of this chapter, you have started to implement the other suggestions of this book in your life. Being empath can be difficult, but now you should at least be feeling more in control because of your grounding techniques, in addition to the ability to block out the negative emotions of others when you can. Even though you may now be at least satisfied with the "goings-on" of your life, you have not yet met your full potential. This chapter will teach you how to overcome fears that hold you back as an empath. You will also learn how to use the power that you have been gifted as an empath so that it brings happiness and fulfillment into your life.

The Benefits of Nurturing Your Inner Empath

If you are struggling with being an empath, it will make sense that you would not want to nurture the power within you. This is especially true if you have not had a lot of positive experiences so far. The truth is, however, that nurturing your inner empath is not making you feel more of the outside world. Nurturing your powers is intended to do the opposite. It will allow you to focus on your own thoughts and feelings. You will also have the ability to focus on another person's feelings instead of feeling everything around you. By doing this, you will learn the skills that the most successful empaths possess. Here are the benefits.

- Trusted- Empaths tend to put out a vibe that people can trust them. A person is more likely to talk to an empath than other people. This also makes it easier for empaths to rise to positions of management. People usually trust that empaths will look out for their own interests, so they are confident in them as leaders.

- Charisma- An empath is usually seen as charismatic, meaning that people are magnetized by our energy. This, with the trust factor, allows us to draw people toward us. It also helps maintain long-term friendships and relationships.

- Diplomatic- Empaths connect well with others. They can read someone's emotions, as well as their motivations, worries, intents, and insecurities. This allows empaths to connect to people on a deep level. They can sense what the people around them need, and by doing that, they can craft their answers, so people receive them easily. They are also skilled at detecting lies and predicting the responses of others. This makes them good at debate.

- Healing- Empaths have the power to heal on an energetic and emotional level. Because we can detect what those around us are feeling, we can train ourselves to read this in a way that we can help them. This is beneficial for bringing families or friends closer together after a misunderstanding or helping someone work through a traumatic experience.

- Crisis management- When empaths learn to manage their abilities, they become great assets in a crisis. Empaths have great minds that can process information quickly. This, when paired with leadership qualities and the ability to direct, helps lower chaos and confusion. People tend to listen, and they can get to safety quicker.

Learning to Overcome Fears
Make Your Own Decisions

Empaths often feel confused or lost. The reason for this is that they spend so much time focusing on all the emotions that are going on around them that they never turn their thoughts inward on themselves. This can make it hard for empaths to find things they are passionate about or that make them happy. So, the next time that you want to go out for fast food or buy a new piece of clothing don't ask for the opinions of your significant other or friend. Instead, buy something based on whether you like it or not. Choose to make food that you like for dinner, instead of asking what everyone else wants. Pick the movie for your next date. As you make your own decisions, you are going to learn more about yourself. You are also going to learn about asserting yourself, which is a step closer to getting the things that you want.

Another part of this is learning to rely on yourself. Have you ever been taken to a party with a friend, become overwhelmed, and then have to stay or find your own way home because they weren't ready to leave? Situations like these can be avoided by planning ahead. You should never make yourself stay somewhere; you are not comfortable. Drive yourself, and if that is not an option, make sure you have money to call for a cab.

Spark Your Creativity

Highly sensitive people make brilliant writers, artists, and musicians of the world. Even if you have never tried to create a work of art or write a story, the gift lies inside you. To overcome your fear of absorbing strong emotions, try to shed them through an art form. When you feel a particularly strong emotion, shed it onto paper through art or words or create a sculpture. Do not allow it to become you, but let it inspire you to create works of art. As you create, imagine all that negativity moving from your body to the work of art. Realize that you have the choice whether you absorb these emotions or let them flow from you.

Challenge Yourself

The only way that you are going to grow your empathic abilities and overcome your fears is to challenge yourself. Immerse yourself in something like feeding the homeless, but do not feel pity or heartache for them. Instead, seek out the warmth and happiness they feel from getting a warm meal. Feel the joy of the other people serving around you, who are also giving back to the community and making a difference. Put yourself in situations that test your boundaries and continue to ground yourself and push back, growing your empathic power. The greater your power is, the more positivity you will be able to draw into your life.

How to Nurture Your Gift for a Better Life
Create Positivity in Your Life

Empaths commonly feel like they should take care of others and try to remedy their negative emotions.
When you do so much for others, however, it is easy to forget about yourself. If you find yourself 'too busy' to take time out to do the things you enjoy, write them in your schedule. Take 20 minutes out of your day to color a picture or an hour to watch your favorite television show. By making yourself happier with life by doing the things that you want, it is only natural that your emotions will follow.

You would be surprised how much a simple smile can bring positive emotions into your life. If you have trouble smiling, go to a mirror. Try to give yourself an authentic smile. After a few tries, start making funny faces at yourself. As you laugh at your contorted image, you will find that authentic smile you are looking for. Try to smile as you go throughout your day. When the neurons in your brain feel a smile, they send out a signal to release 'happy' chemicals that enhance the positive feelings of your mind.

Seek Positive Experiences and People in Your Life
As an empath, you have the incredible power to attract positive things to your life. You can seek out the people and situations that you want to be around. You can quit a job that makes you unhappy and finds something more fulfilling. You can change your living situation, your romantic situation, essentially, your entire life.

Learning what is healthiest for you is not always as easy as an empath. Sometimes, you may find that your familiar routines and even your relationships should be avoided to preserve your mental health. This does not mean that you have to drop your toxic friend for good, but you should probably limit your time around them and talking to them. Instead, start finding positive situations to involve yourself in and positive people to be around. Avoid stressful things like going to a crowded club or party in favor of quieter, more relaxing settings. Cultivate friends who focus on the good in others. Find people at work who are always looking for the positive and keep them close.

You can also add positivity through the media that you consume. Listen to uplifting songs and absorb innovative, joyous works of art. Choose happier movies, books, and television shows. You can even put positive art up around your home or create posters with hopeful words.

Learn to Tune into Specific Feelings in the World Around You

So far, these tips should have helped you create a positive environment that creates happiness in your life. This is important, so you are prepared for this step. Something that you should note is that this part of your journey may take years to master. Once you have mastered it, however, you will find your calling. The end of this step is the self-awareness of your purpose.

If we have a strong connection to someone, we sense their feelings above others. This is because our mind recognizes their energy. We are already receptive to them because we are close to them. Even then, however, we sometimes have trouble separating their feelings from our own. By learning this technique, you will learn to break that strong connection so you can focus on their feelings and helping them. You will also be able to do this with strangers, should you choose to.

To open yourself to a specific person, you must create a receptive space in yourself. It is advised that you practice this meditation many times before you try it with someone else. Start by sitting in an area where you can be alone and meditate. Start by deep breathing as you try to clear your mind. Then, picture your roots growing out of yourself and grounding you to the earth. Feel that strong self of self-awareness within.

As the core of your self-awareness remains strong, choose an anchor. This is a representation of something that ties you to this earth. Slowly practice relaxing your toes, feet, ankles, calves, knees, and thighs, followed by your fingers, hands, arms, shoulders, and torso. Then imagine your head and neck relaxing completely. Feel the heaviness of your body and feel grounded to the earth. Imagine the globe floating, like a giant anchor in your mind. Keep imagining this, deep breathing while you imagine your body dissolving and becoming only your self-awareness.

Once you are completely grounded, start to open yourself. Imagine your tree blooming, its branches opening up to receive what may come. Then, focus on a single thought. While you are practicing, focus on the thought of calmness or peace. Open yourself to receive that.

You can use this exercise to open yourself to others as well. Once you have mastered it, you will be able to focus on a single person and know what they are feeling. You can use this information to respond to them or to prepare a response for what they are going to say. In many cases, you will find yourself able to pinpoint what someone needs to hear and quickly help them solve their trauma.

CHAPTER 12:

Empathic Self-Care Tips

"The deeper your self-love, the greater your protection."

Danielle Laporte

Self-care, as an Empath is essential. When you are an Empath, knowing how to rest, recharge, and cleanse your energies can promote a more fluid sense of well-being. These activities can release any energies you may be carrying, as well as produce a greater strength within you so that you can prevent unwanted energies from clinging to you in the first place. Stress and a poor self-care routine can easily result in individuals acquiring unwanted or harmful energies in the first place. So, reducing these and taking care of yourself can minimize the occurrence of this.

Here are some things that you need to begin doing to take care of your energies and keep yourself feeling nourished and supported.

Re-Charge Often

Recharging is an important way to keep your energies full. For an Empath, recharging often happens in nature or through direct rest. When you go into nature, connecting to the elements of the Earth around, you can be highly supportive in allowing you to release any unwanted energies and refuel yourself with positive, beneficial energies. Many Empaths report feeling drawn to the forest often, regularly retreating to the forest to find peace and comfort. Some Empaths even recognize the word forest as meaning "for rest."

In addition to relaxing in nature and connecting with the elements, true rest through the form of sleeping can be deeply nourishing for an Empath. You can also spend time with your pets if you have any (which most Empaths do) as they seem to have a deep knowledge over how they can support you in feeling nourished and whole. The unconditional love shared between you, and your pets are truly nourishing when spending time together.

Many Empaths who are not actively caring for themselves well through recharging frequently will find themselves having disturbed sleep, either not sleeping enough or struggling to stay asleep all night long. This comes from the chronic stress they are facing. By intentionally creating a stronger sleep routine and getting more sleep, Empaths can support themselves in feeling nourished and recharged so that they can go out and face the next day with confidence and ease.

Exercise Your Creativity

Despite Empaths being highly creative, some will actually shut down their creativity. This may occur from their childhood being abused or bullied around their creative talents, or it may occasionally happen if they are feeling overwhelmed and are struggling to dedicate enough time and attention toward creative outlets.

If you are someone who shuts down your creativity to avoid being bullied or hurt, it is a good idea to begin exploring and exercising your creativity once more.

This process can help you awaken your energies again and begin expressing yourself in ways that you have denied for a long time. Even just starting with something as easy as coloring is a great way to get started. Then, over time, you can move into your preferred mediums of creativity so that you can begin expressing yourself in the ways that feel best to you.

If you are in a funk and it has caused you to refrain from creating recently due to any number of excuses, recognize that the most likely reason is that you are struggling actually to express yourself. For Empaths, the artwork is an essential form of self-expression. Naturally, if you stop creating, it is important to look into the reason why. Then, you can begin to heal the block and practice creating again. Sometimes, it is as simple as setting aside some time, putting some music on and just doing it.

Consider Working for Yourself
Working for yourself as an Empath can be a powerful form of self-care. Being able to set your own hours and choose your own rules is empowering and can

support you in having a positive work environment that enables you to create an income while feeling inspired and empowered to do so. Furthermore, if you feel a deep calling toward something in particular, such as healing or creating, you can create your own business doing just that. This means that not only do you free yourself from the restraints and toxicity of corporate jobs, but you also enable yourself to do what feels the best for you. This can have an even greater impact on your overall health than you may think, so be sure to consider it!

If you cannot leave your job or work for yourself does not seem reasonable at this time, consider going into business for yourself part-time. Even just creating artwork and selling it online or performing healing services here and there can be a great way to exercise your freedom, tap into your gift, and feel like you are gaining the benefits of working for yourself without losing some of the benefits that come with working for someone else.

Practice Energy Clearing Often

Energy clearing is an absolute must. When you are an Empath, energy clearing goes much beyond basic self-care. This is not just about feeling good but about actually releasing energies that may be preventing you from doing so. Daily energy clearing practices, such as meditation or binaural beats, are extremely important. You should also have stronger antidotes on hand for those times when you feel that you are carrying an excess of energy and you need freedom from it. These "stronger dose medicines" of energy clearing are ones that may take longer but will have a great impact on supporting your healing.

Meditate

Meditating is a powerful way of supporting yourself in clearing unwanted energies. Meditating for just ten minutes a day has been said to have a strong impact on supporting you in clearing all that you do not desire to carry with you, freeing your mind so that you can experience more peace and joy in the present moment.

If you find meditating to be challenging, you might consider using guided meditations or music to support you in your meditation practice. Additionally, you may want to start with meditating for just a couple of minutes at a time, then gradually increasing the amount of time you are meditating until you reach ten minutes per day. This can make it easier for you to build this practice and support it in your daily life.

Hot Showers

Hot showers have a great ability to support you in releasing unwanted energies from your body. Using the hot water to cleanse and purify your body while envisioning all of the unwanted energies going down the drain can be very powerful in energy cleansing. Some people also use bath products that are infused with energy-cleansing materials, such as sage, Himalayan salt, or various essential oils to support them in releasing energies. You can also find soaps that are infused with crystals that clear energies, too.

Himalayan Salt Baths

Himalayan salt is said to be great for drawing out

toxins from the body, supporting you in releasing any energies that may be stored within your body and cells that are preventing you from clearing your energies effectively. If you do not have access to Himalayan salt, Epsom salts, dead sea salts, and Celtic sea salts are also excellent alternatives.

Binaural Beats

Binaural beats are a form of energetic music designed to support you in attuning yourself to certain energy frequencies. They can promote healing and balance, release energies, and support you in attuning you to virtually any frequency you desire. If you are clearing energies, using a binaural beat specific to clearing energies can be valuable. 536Hz and 432Hz are known to be good ones for energy clearing.

Get Energy Healing Done

If you are feeling particularly overloaded and like you need more support in releasing a great deal of energy, having an energy healing done by a healer can be powerful. Getting reiki or another energy clearing method done by a certified practitioner or Shaman can support you in releasing energies by bringing the skilled hand of a practitioner on board to help you. Think of it as a message for your aura!

Clear Your Chakras

Chakras are energy meridians within the body that support various types of energies. We typically recognize seven energy chakras within the body: the root chakra by your tail bone, the sacral chakra by your navel, the solar plexus chakra just below your rib cage, your heart chakra in the center of your chest, your throat chakra in the upper part of your throat, your third eye chakra in the center of your forehead, and your crown chakra directly above the crown of your head. Each of these chakras represents a specific type of energy and needs to be balanced in order to maintain a positive energy flow.

Here is a basic cheat sheet to help you understand and balance the chakras:

- Root Chakra: associated with the color red.

Grounding, eating deep red foods, walking on the grass barefooted and wearing the color red can support you in balancing this chakra.

- Sacral Chakra: associated with the color orange. Creativity, exercise, eating orange foods, and wearing the color orange can support you in balancing this chakra.

- Solar Plexus Chakra: associated with the color yellow. Building your confidence and self-esteem, reaching goals, eating yellow and citrusy foods, and wearing the color yellow can support you in balancing this chakra.

- Heart Chakra: associated with the color green. Opening your heart, healing your emotional body, and doing things that engage you in the energies of love and compassion, as well as eating green foods and wearing the color green can support you in balancing this chakra.

- Throat Chakra: associated with the color blue. Speaking your truth, confidence in saying what you mean, eating blue foods, and wearing the color blue can support you in balancing this chakra.

- Third Eye Chakra: associated with the color indigo. Meditations that open your third eye, daydreaming, awakening your Empathic abilities, eating foods that are indigo and wearing the color indigo can support you in balancing this chakra.

- Crown Chakra: associated with the color violet. Praying, meditating, connecting to source, eating foods that are violet and wearing the color violet can support you in balancing this chakra.

In addition to these basic practices, you can also incorporate many other things such as essential oils, yoga, guided meditations, Reiki, and other practices in clearing and balancing these chakra energies.

Practice A Healthy Social Life

Engaging in a healthy social life and practicing positive activities is important for an Empath. Make sure that you are surrounding yourself with the right people who genuinely have your best interest at heart. You should also make sure that they are focused on assisting you in creating your best life possible.

Find and spend time with friends who will enjoy doing activities such as creating, attending positive social events, and engaging in activities such as yoga and meditation with you. While not all of your friends need to have these activities in common with you, having some that are willing to embrace your Empath path with you and join in on these activities can assist you in feeling supported and empowered by your friends.

Make sure that if you do have friends who are not entirely supportive that you minimize your time with them. You might have friends who are not entirely supportive, not because they are abusive, but because they simply do not understand and relate. While you do not need to discard these friends, be mindful of how their beliefs and behavior impacts you and make sure that you refrain from spending too much time with them if they are having a negative impact on you. Do regular check-ins to make sure that your friends are positive influences in your life and that you feel happy, supported, and empowered around them.

Thanks to the internet, you also have access to many online support forums and groups where you can connect with fellow Empaths around the world. This may even help you link up with local Empaths who understand you and can support each other. Take advantage of the resources available to you and be sure to find people who assist you in living your best life possible. Even if you naturally lean toward introverted tendencies, having a few people who you come out of your shell around and who you genuinely enjoy can be extremely beneficial to your overall wellbeing.

Take Advantage of To Do Lists

Any Empath who has not grown up educated on how

to take care of themselves properly may find themselves feeling overwhelmed and even struggling to cope with feeling like a failure. This comes from having a lowered self-esteem and a sense of self-confidence. As such, setting and accomplishing goals can be extremely fulfilling for Empaths. This can also be a great way to bypass the mundaneness of routines and still get everything done.

Creating a to-do list each morning is a great way to provide yourself with a series of mini-goals that you desire to accomplish each day. Then, as you check things off the list, you will begin to feel fulfilled and satisfied. This can support you in having a deep sense of fulfillment, which is essential for Empaths. It can also support you in raising your self-esteem and self-confidence and in feeling more capable of achieving and accomplishing all that you desire to do.

In addition to creating daily to-do lists, it is wise to set weekly and monthly goals as well. These can provide you with larger goals that give you the opportunity to have even greater accomplishment in your life. The more you check off of these lists, the better you will feel. Thus, you will begin to feel far more positive and better about yourself. This is both a great way to set aside all-day routines while still getting things done, and to feel great. For an Empath, this can even support you in breaking a mood swing or coming out of an energy funk so that you can begin to enjoy life once again.

Have a Gratitude Journal

Gratitude is a powerful energy that can support in recognizing and highlighting the parts of our lives that we love and enjoy. Keeping a gratitude journal can be a great way to support yourself in feeling better and caring for your energy. When you use a gratitude journal, you train your brain to focus on the positive in addition to the negative. It also allows you to reframe the negative. It is a great way to begin to see the silver lining and to develop a sense of optimism.

If you have never used a gratitude journal, you can start now by purchasing a journal and committing to writing in it daily or weekly, whatever suits you best. You can journal, brain dump, use bullet points, or otherwise write down what you are grateful for in any way that feels right for you. As long as you are consistent, you will find that it works great and supports you by promoting a more uplifted mood and a general sense of wellbeing. You should also write in your gratitude journal whenever you have a small win or celebratory moment in your life. Even giving thanks to the Universe is a great practice.

The other powerful thing about practicing gratitude is that it re-wires your brain to an appreciative and optimistic perspective. Over time by practicing this skill, you will notice you will have many more things to be grateful for.

CHAPTER 13:

Exercises for Empaths

Now that you are aware of what goes into being an empath, it is time to share some exercises that will be helpful with your abilities to grow your powers. Being aware and accepting of your abilities is the first step, but now it is time for you to learn some practical exercises that will help you maintain your powers in a healthy way. Though we are lucky to have these abilities, they can quickly become burdens if we unmanaged them properly.

Exercise is an important word to understand when it comes to defining your abilities. Upon first reading that word, your mind might first go to a place of physical exercise, like jogging or doing push-ups. For empaths, it is important that they put an emphasis on exercising their mind. If there isn't a focus on expanding your thoughts and ability to understand others, then you will only be at a consistent level of empathy, not using your powers to their fullest abilities.

There are some things that are going to work better for growing different parts of your mind, so make sure that you understand what you are good at so you know what to "work out." Think of it just like you would your body. You might want to tone-up your arms, or maybe your concern would be slimming down your stomach. You would then come up with an exercise regimen targeted specifically at those areas. To determine what you need to work out, look at common thought patterns, and consistent anxieties. Your weak areas might be the parts that you want to work out the most.

Sometimes, you might need to include a professional into your healing or exercising. This might be a more experienced and knowledgeable empath, or it could be a psychiatrist to help with any medication you might feel you could benefit from. Seeing a professional isn't a sign of weakness. It is important to admit when you need a little more help and not to be fearful that you might not be able to do it all alone. You do not need to use this form of professional help forever, but it can be useful when you first start to grow your abilities.

Crystals and plants can help to grow your abilities as well, so it is a good idea to have these around. They are things that come from the earth, so it is helpful in keeping you grounded. Being grounded is a mentality that you have to work on, but when you can't do it all in your head, these physical symbols will help.
Holding certain types of crystals and being surrounded by specific plants can help remind you that you are connected with the earth.

Meditation
Meditation is going to be a very helpful tool when growing your empath abilities. The goal of meditation is to reach a state where your mind is calm and empty, and your body relaxed. Meditation is commonly thought of to be a religious practice or one that involves specific positions or areas to do so. It is much more generic of a term, and there are no strict rules or guidelines for how you should meditate.

Mediation takes practice, so set some time aside every day to work on this. At first, it might be a bit uncomfortable. You might only be able to meditate for a few minutes before your mind starts to wander back towards different anxieties again. Do not be discouraged if it doesn't go well the first few times, or even within the first few weeks.

Find a place that you can specifically associate with meditation. If you try to meditate in a place that you do other things, then you might find it is difficult to focus on anything other than the activities you normally do in that area. For example, do not expect to meditate on your couch where you normally watch TV or sit on your phone; when you try to meditate, you'll just start to think about what you might be missing on TV or get the urge to pull out your phone.

Do not let anyone interrupt or encroach on your meditation place. Make it your own. If you live in a small space, it is not like you have to dedicate an entire area to meditation. When you might struggle to fit all your stuff in one place, you do not have to be expected to keep a separate place to meditate. Instead, just make a certain spot dedicated only to meditation. It might just be the opposite side of the couch that you normally sit on. Or instead of using your bed, use a spot on the floor right next to your bed.

Find ways to meditate as well quickly, so you can do it even when you are away from your meditation space. Sometimes, you might need a break at work, so you can meditate on your lunch break. It could involve a spot in the workroom, a grassy area outside, or even the back seat of your car. The more you practice meditation, the easier it will be to get into this mindset when you need to the most.

When you expose yourself to too many sensory overloads, it can be challenging for you to find yourself, meaning a loss of your emotional control. If you are stressed about what happened in the morning, overwhelmed with the tasks you have to do now, and anxious about the things you are doing later in the day, your mind will easily start to overload. On top of that, empaths have to deal with the feelings that they are picking up from other people. Meditation can help to wipe your mind clean so you can focus only on what you have to in order to get through the present moment.

Realigning Energies

When our energies are not balanced, it can make everything feel out of whack. This is something that we have to check often. If you had a particularly bad week, it doesn't mean your life is over, but you have to realign your energy so that you can get off the next week to the right start, rather than carrying over the negative energy that was created the week before.

You have to make sure that you are even controlling some of your positive energies. If you continue to feed only off of positive energy and choose to disregard the negative completely, you might find yourself crashing. You have to stay realistic and make sure you are resolving the negativity rather than just trying to suppress it. Do not pretend like everything is okay when it is not. Energy isn't going to dissolve.

It might disappear momentarily, but only for it to show in some other form. For example, imagine having an issue with a close friend or romantic partner. Instead of bringing it up, you ignore it, hoping to avoid an argument. However, the same issue comes up again, and this time, you are twice as mad. That negative energy reappeared and actually multiplied, when it could have been resolved, had you confronted the other person in the first place.

In order to realign them, you have to identify them. The source of negative energy will not always be immediately obvious. For a trained empath, the energy will be easier to spot, but at first, it is going to be always challenging to pinpoint what the root issue or deeper problem is. Life will not always be an equal balance of positive and negative energy. It is not as though you have to seek out the negativity to keep yourself aligned. You just have to make sure that you are not ignoring anything that needs to be resolved. If the negative energy truly doesn't exist around you, consider yourself a lucky one. However, do not let your mind convince itself that there's no negative energy when it is sitting right in front of you.

Always seek the balance. When you are feeling particularly negative, remember that it might be a perspective brought on by the challenging times. When one bad thing happens after another, it can start to feel like everything in your life is difficult. Do not also forget to identify the good things that are happening. It is not about just "positive thinking" or "looking on the bright side." Search for a balance, because there usually is one.

Once you have practiced how to put them back in place, it will be harder for them to become disrupted again. When you have control over your energies and know how to maintain them, then you will find that the balance doesn't become disrupted easily again.

Connecting to the Earth

Grounding is very important for empaths. Grounding involves connecting oneself back to the earth. In a world where we live on the twenty-seventh floor of an apartment building surrounded by hundreds of other people with cell phones constantly around us and other technology always buzzing, it can be easy to forget that our ancestors once lived in mud huts and caves. We can start to think like computers easier than we do animals, and when an empath does this, they start to lose their abilities to feel what others do. In order to make sure that we are staying close to who we are at the core, we have to stay grounded.

Spending time outside is crucial for empaths. Not only is it good to stay connected to nature, but the vitamin D from the sun can prevent low moods and even depression.

When you can't get outside, make sure to bring the outdoors into your home. Surround yourself with plants and take the time to grow things from seeds. Care for nature, even if it is through your pet. Having an animal companion can help you remember some of your natural tendencies, such as the will for food, warmth, and friendship.

Water is helpful for grounding you as well. When it is raining gently, open your window to hear the water wash over the earth. Take baths as a form of relaxation. Drink plenty of water to help it nourish your body from within.

Activate your senses with things associated with the earth. Use natural scents in your home and surround yourself with herbs. Eat enough fruits and vegetables and things made from scratch rather than foods always out of a container. Do as much as you can to remind yourself of the wonderful earth we live on.

Self-Care

Self-care is dire for those that are empaths. Empaths have the need to make sure everyone else is taken care of before they do so themselves. This is a great quality to have, but when not managed, can mean overlooking your own feelings. In order to make sure that someone is still taking care of us, we have to set time apart for self-care. This involves basic things, such as proper hygiene, nutrition, and healthy exposure to positive activities. It means nurturing talents and encouraging moments of creativity and individuality. We have to take care of ourselves as we would a pet that we own, or even the same way that we take care of certain objects, or our household. You might spend hours-a-day cleaning your house or picking up after kids, but when's the last time you took more than a quick shower? When's the last time you took time to put as much effort into taking care of yourself as you do taking care of everything else?

Make sure to identify the things that you enjoy. This might be something as simple as watching reruns of a certain TV show, or it could be a more extensive activity like rock climbing. Set a time every week that you can do this with no interruptions. Put as much importance on this as you would a doctor's appointment or a job interview. Treat these moments of self-care like they are appointments you can't miss.

Things as simple as taking a shower or remembering your medication can even be classified as self-care. Many parents know how difficult it can be to find some time alone. You might only eat the leftover scraps from your child's meal or skip showers so that they do not have to be alone for too long. When we stop taking care of ourselves, we start to lose ourselves. When this is done, we become out of touch with our own emotions, which will make it even more challenging to read the emotions of others.

Get to know yourself like you would a friend. Instead of only thinking about what you have to do next or how you might have to help someone else, make sure that you are still staying in touch with who you are, having deep conversations and questioning your beliefs.

Never treat yourself like you would an enemy. Do not punish yourself or put yourself in uncomfortable scenarios as a form of self-harm. When we picture self-harm, it is usually in the form of an eating disorder or cutting. Self-harm can emerge in other ways as well, so we have to make sure that we are not torturing ourselves because we believe that we deserve punishment.

Use as much empathy on yourself as you are for other individuals.

Creating Boundaries

Creating boundaries is crucial for those that are empaths. We might feel like the weight of the world is on our shoulders, so as a reaction, we'll often do what we can to help other people. Sometimes, this means that we might end up doing things we do not want to or things that make us uncomfortable, all for the sake of helping out another individual. Boundaries are important so that we do not push ourselves too far.

Boundaries are not set in stone forever, either. Sometimes, we do not want to say "no" because we think that it will end up putting us in a permanent negative situation. Remember that you can lower your boundaries as you grow as an empath, so if you need to be strict in the beginning, that is perfectly fine.

A good first step for boundary setting is learning when to say no. If someone is asking you to help them in a way that makes you uncomfortable, or hurts you in any way, then that is not fair of them. If they get mad at you for saying "no," then that is on them, not on you. As an empath, you will feel the need to help more than others will, but this doesn't mean that it is your responsibility to help.

This also means speaking up for yourself and letting others know when you might be uncomfortable. Do not let others take advantage of you, and when you feel as though you are unfairly treated, stand up for yourself. This might be difficult for empaths to learn how to do. You might have gone through your life being more passive, wanting to help others when you saw them suffer. Now is your time to reclaim yourself, not letting anyone walk all over you. Be strong and resilient and do not do anything that you do not want to do.

If people do not like "the new you," or a person that says no and speaks up for themselves, consider that these people are not the type that you should include in your life. You might have been a "yes man" all your life, and that attracted certain types of people. Then, as you start to say "no" more often, these people start to go away. If that is the case, remember that there's nothing wrong with you. You are better-off without users or manipulators anyway.

Putting Yourself First

We have talked a lot about making yourself a priority. That is because it is an idea that seems foreign to empaths and will often be overlooked. It seems nobler in our society to be self-sacrificing, and we should all aim to be people that help others. However, this can also cause the person that is doing so much some serious damage if they do not take good care of themselves. So no matter how noble you wish to be, never fail to put yourself first.

Some people will be uncomfortable when doing this. Especially if you are a caregiver of any sort, you know that it can be challenging to put yourself before others. It is crucial that you do so, however, or else you'll eventually get to a point where you can't help anyone else at all.

We often see this as a narcissistic tendency or one that seems selfish. It is true that if we all only focused on ourselves forever, there would be a lot less good in the world. Our society thrives because of so many people's willingness to help others. However, if we all only focused on other people and never ourselves, we would all be exhausted as well.

Think of how flight attendants emphasize the importance of putting your own mask on first when confronted with an accident in the air. The oxygen masks drop from the ceiling, and you are advised to put your own mask on before putting the mask on the people next to you, should they need help. This idea seems absurd to some people; you might worry that the children next to you would suffocate before you got their mask on. However, if you first put theirs on, you will not make it in time to put your own on, and then the children might suffocate anyway.

Conclusion

Having empathic abilities can be very challenging; however, with a greater understanding of your skills, you will be able to control their impact on your life more effectively. Furthermore, by implementing the methods discussed in this book for becoming more grounded, you will be able to avoid the pitfalls that many empaths encounter as a result of letting their abilities go unchecked.

Hopefully, this book has provided you with the tools you need to get the most from your empathic abilities. The very best of luck to you as you begin living the life of a truly empowered empath!

Mindfulness Meditation For Beginners

The Ultimate and Easy Guide to Learn How to Create Inner Peace, Happiness, and Declutter Your Mind. Techniques to Improve Health and Increase Your Mental Power

Deniel Clark

Description

If you are upset because you lost a competition that you were enthusiastic about winning, you do not label your sadness as something 'negative,' but carefully observe it and feel it without overthinking it. This can help you to quickly understand and then slowly let go of the emotion without overthinking or over-reacting to it. Had you felt it was something negative, you would have likely held on to it for long, which may have made it turn into some form of mild depression.

Therefore, meditation can instill in you the awareness of being in the present and accepting everything that comes with it openly, happily and nonjudgmentally.

This is known as mindfulness and precisely what meditation cultivates in us. When you live in the moment, you stop rehashing the past and all your failures, setbacks and mistakes it holds; neither do you panic about the future and what problems it will bring with itself. Not just that, but you do not spend hours daydreaming about a very happy future or even keep recalling the good old memories.

This is a beginner's guide to mindfulness meditation, and you will be able to learn the following:

- History of Meditation
- How Meditation Works
- Benefits of Mindfulness and Meditation
- Different Kinds of Meditation
- How to prepare for meditation
- Techniques to Practice Mindfulness Meditation
- How Meditation Helps Reduce Stress and Anxiety
- Declutter Your Mind
- Mindful Meditative Practice and Simple Exercise Examples
- Cultivating mindfulness into daily life

By the time you are done reading this book, you will have discovered a newfound zest for life and will be motivated to live better by meditating regularly.

Introduction

While looking inside yourself with the idea of finding an untapped well of inner peace and tranquility might seem daunting at first, rest assured that it is something anyone can achieve if they dedicate time and mental energy to practice mindfulness meditation every day. What's more, after you get the basics down you will find that almost any situation easily lends itself to being mindful if you simply commit yourself to be fully present at the moment and open yourself completely to the signals that your body is sending you.

While one of the best things about mindfulness meditation is its malleable nature, when you are first getting started, it is recommended that you set some time aside each day to devote to the practice specifically. Ideally, this should be someplace that is quiet and during a period of time when you feel relaxed and where you can devote as much as thirty minutes to going deep within yourself without fear of worldly distractions. Remember, being mindful is all about creating space between the sensory information that your body is always sending to your mind and your reactions to that information so the less stimuli you have to deal with at the start, the easier you will find the practice to be.

Getting started

1. Choose a set time and stick to it: As with any burgeoning habit, it is important that you create a routine for your mindfulness meditation and stay with it if you hope for the practice to stick. It typically takes 30 days for a new habit of taking root in your daily schedule which is why it is important to commit fully to practicing mindfulness meditation if you ever want it to become part of your routine. Due to its low impact nature, nothing external is required, it is very easy for many people to make excuses to get out of meditating, especially if their daily schedule is already filled to bursting.

If you find yourself frequently coming up with an excuse to get out of meditating at the moment, you may find the following piece of advice particularly useful. "Practice mindfulness meditation for fifteen minutes every day unless, of course, you are extremely busy in which case you should practice for thirty minutes instead." Don't let the outside world intrude on your potential for inner peace, find a time each day that works for you and sticking with it no matter what; in a month's time, you will be glad you did.

2. Get started by focusing on the moment: While the ultimate goal of mindfulness meditation is to quiet the mind in an effort to find a state of internal calm despite the hustle and bustle of the outside world, many people find it difficult to achieve this state right out of the gate. Instead, you will likely find it easier to start to supplant any thoughts you might have by focusing all of your attention on the signals that your senses are relaying to you to the exclusion of everything else. While you might not feel as though you are receiving much data on the physical world, especially if you are practicing in a quiet, temperate space, the truth of the matter is that your brain naturally filters out approximately eighty percent of

everything it receives, you just need to get in the habit of tapping into it.

With practice, you will learn to tune out your more common thoughts and to instead tune into what is going on around you. When you do this, it is important to simply take in the information your senses are providing without thinking about it too deeply or passing judgement on what you perceive. Judging tends to lead to additional thoughts or, even worse, comparison of the present group of situations to those of the past which is more likely to pull you out of the moment and make finding the state of calm you are looking for even more difficult than it is likely to be, especially when you are just getting started.

Remember, the goal with mindfulness meditation is to get as close to existing at the moment as possible and ignoring everything outside of your current surroundings as much as possible. To reach the required state, you are going to want to start by focusing on your breathing, the feel of the air slowly entering and exiting your lungs as well as any smells or tastes that go along with this practice. From there you can then expand the sphere of observation to any other sensations that your body might be experiencing, all the while going deeper into yourself in search of the point where your mind ceases to form new thoughts and simply exists in a state of peaceful relaxation.

3. Make an effort to avoid judging what you feel: When you first begin practicing mindfulness meditation it is perfectly natural for your mind to intrude with thoughts about your current surroundings or to fill the void you are trying to achieve with a constant stream of consciousness. This occurs because, over the years, you have trained your brain to constantly be moving from one thought to the next in a rush to reach some conclusion or another.

When you find these errant thoughts breaching your sense of mental calm, it is important to not interact with them as much as possible and instead to let them simply float away without interacting with them. If you find yourself getting sidetracked, it is important to not attach a judgment to what has happened and to center yourself once more and continue as before instead simply. While this step is the most difficult for many people, it is important to keep it up until it becomes second nature as any interaction with the stray thoughts, even if it is just to chastise yourself for getting off track is an easy way to let even more thoughts through which will make it more difficult to find the state of mind that you are looking for.

4. Keep at it: When you first begin practicing mindfulness meditation, it is important to do so with the right level of expectations regarding your results. Specifically, you will want to keep in mind that your mind is likely to wander frequently and that you will need to persevere through these periods if you are ever going to reach the level of mental quiet that you are looking for. To understand the ultimate mindset that you are striving for, you may find it helpful to consider the period of blankness the mind enters after a question has been asked, but before the answer comes to you. Finding a way to reach this type of state

is key to your long-term success.

When it comes to clearing the mind, some people find it helpful to visualize their thoughts as a stream of bubbles that they are watching flow past them; others visualize a gate coming down to block out the stream of consciousness entirely leaving the thoughts to pile up on the far side. While these visualizations can make it easier to be aware of stray thoughts without interacting with them it is important not to become too reliant on them as they are still thoughts, and you ultimately want to do away with them once your mind has gotten used to the idea that it doesn't need to be moving from one thought or another constantly. However you manage it, it is important to not to worry about chastising yourself when stray thoughts do emerge and to instead simply acknowledge the lapse and then get back to what you were doing.

CHAPTER 1

History of Meditation

Meditation has been around for centuries and is believed to be a very ancient practice. In fact, it is the very practice that helped Buddha understand himself and attain nirvana, which is the highest state of enlightenment and contentment.

Let me take you on a journey of how meditation came into being in this chapter.

Some of the oldest and earliest written records related to meditation are the scriptures of Vedantism, which was a part of Hindu tradition around 1500 BCE (before Common Era). Meditation was practiced in various traditions, cultures, and religions and is believed to be an integral element of the most ancient Vedic and Hindu tradition. It is in between the 4th and 6th centuries BCE that the Buddhist and Chinese Taoist traditions started developing their own unique and diverse versions of meditation. In the west, meditation was primarily worked on and developed by Saint Augestine, Philo of Alexandria and the Desert Fathers of Middle East.

The word 'meditation' comes from the Latin word 'meditatum,' which means 'to reflect on something.' Despite the availability of certain ancient scriptures related to meditation, researchers are still unsure of the exact time when the practice of meditation started. However, many archaeological findings suggest that our ancestors meditated when they started hunting. It is believed that they then passed on their knowledge to their descendants who then transferred it to their progenies and the cycle then carried on. It is believed that meditation began in the Eastern countries, primarily due to its association with Buddha. Buddha was a noble prince who then turned into a monk and lived in Southeast Asia over 2600 years ago. He was upset with the way sufferings ruled the world and how people were engulfed in worldly gains and pleasures, which made him abandon his luxurious life in the palace and search for the true meaning of life and peace. He finally attained it by discovering the noble eightfold path, which leads to enlightenment by meditating under a tree.

Buddhists and those who are impressed with the teachings of Buddha use meditation to develop a heightened sense of awareness and attain nirvana (enlightenment). After Buddha, several Buddhist and Hindu scholars and monks worked on meditation and created many versions of it, one of which is Zen. Zen is a popular meditation practice carried out commonly in Japan.

After meditation became popular in Burma, Thailand, Tibet, Indonesia, China, Japan, India, and other Southeast Asian countries, it then moved to the west. The earliest texts related to meditation and the western world date back to the nineteenth century, and at that time, it was primarily the domain of missionaries and scholars. However, it was in the middle of the twentieth century that meditation started gaining more prominence in western countries. As more people from the western countries traveled to the eastern side and took an interest in spirituality and mindfulness, they became aware of the power of meditation and introduced it to the western culture.

Currently, Dr. Jon Kabat-Zinn and Deepak Chopra are two of the most influential and popular figures in the sphere of meditation and mindfulness today and have carried out extensive work on the subject.

By virtue that you are reading this book, it is clear that meditation certainly did travel the whole world, and now it has reached your doorstep.

CHAPTER 2

Benefits of Mindfulness

Mindfulness meditation has been around for years, used by all types of people in all kinds of different situations. However, the benefits of mindfulness have not been properly proven by science until recently. Mindfulness meditation is considered an ancient practice, but that has not stopped it from becoming popular amongst many big businesses and companies, as well as many individuals and families.

Mindfulness has become so popular because of the ability to do it anywhere. Mindfulness meditation can be done by the sink while washing the dishes; at work in the middle of the meeting; or even while making dinner for the family. It's the practice of awareness. Mindfulness allows you to be aware of the past, present, and the future, but it helps you focus on remaining in the moment. Putting all of your attention on the present makes your life easier in so many ways.

The practice of mindfulness, when kept consistent, can rewire our brains and allow us to reap many rewards. The benefits are plenty, and they can affect anyone of any age, from young children to the elderly. Here is a list of the many proven benefits:

Benefits to Mental Health
01. Mindfulness Meditation reduces anxiety;

It has been proven that a single session of mindfulness can reduce anxiety levels by a significant amount. Studies have been done, and researchers have found that after a mindfulness meditation session, people who had high levels of anxiety have improvements in anxiety levels.

In modern times our daily lives, at home or at work, requires us to focus on anything bad that has happened in the past and think ahead to anything that can go wrong in the coming future. This way of thinking makes it easy for us to miss what's happening in the present, and it leads to higher levels of anxiety, especially in working people.

In 2013 there was a study of 93 individuals in the Massachusetts General Hospital. These individuals were all diagnosed with generalized anxiety. The study was an 8-week long group intervention that had the individuals focused on stress management based on mindfulness meditation. The study found that the groups that went through this mindfulness stress management had a significant reduction in their anxiety levels.

2. Mindfulness Meditation can lower your stress levels;

In today's society, anxiety and stress have become an everyday influence on our lives. Cortisol is known as the stress hormone, and in this modern, fast-paced world, our bodies are thrown into overdrive producing this hormone. Mindfulness meditation can help us learn how to control our stress levels by letting us focus on the present instead of worry about what tomorrow will bring. There are 47 clinical trials that found improvements in the stress levels of patients and reduced levels of cortisol.

3. Mindfulness Meditation decreases distractions

You go into the kitchen to wash the dishes, but before you can get started, you remember that you need to take out mince for dinner. You go to the fridge to take out the mince, and you notice that there isn't any milk and you might need some in the morning for breakfast or for a late-night drink. You grab your keys and go to the store. On your way to the store, you see a specialist for a carwash, and you think that your car is quite dirty, so you decide to wait an hour for your car to get cleaned. Then on your way home, you buy some milk and other groceries you remember you need.

When you finally get home, you put the milk in the fridge and realize you haven't taken the mince out yet. Now it's too late, and the mince won't defrost in time to make dinner, and that's when you turn around and see the sink filled with the dirty dishes you were supposed to clean.

These are distractions, and our lives are filled with them. The practice of mindfulness meditation helps us focus our attention and cut out all the distraction of everyday life. This was proven in a Harvard study where participants were put through a mindfulness program that lasted for eight weeks. At the end of the study, the participants that went through the mindfulness meditation showed significant improvement in their ability to avoid distractions compared to the control group that did not undergo any form of mindfulness meditation.

4. Mindfulness Meditation improves your attention span;

It's no surprise that Mindfulness meditation improves your ability to hold your attention on something. It decreases your chances of getting distracted and therefore improves your attention span. Although the modern world is filled with distractions, it also requires our full attention in order to get even the simplest of tasks done. This is why there are so many incidents of people failing to complete their work in time or students missing deadlines on their assignments. Mindfulness meditation is the perfect daily habit to increase your attention and allow you to focus on the tasks that need to be done instead of short-term distractions.

5. Mindfulness Meditation helps people to prevent depression relapse and cope with symptoms;

There are many studies and research proving the benefits of Mindfulness-based cognitive therapy to prevent depression and help cope with the symptoms. Some people who have suffered from depression are prone to relapses and mindfulness meditation can help prevent that.

One study done in 2011 found Mindfulness-based cognitive therapy was effective for preventing depression relapse in patients with Major Depressive Disorder. There is also a study that found Mindfulness-based cognitive therapy helped prevent patients with a history of childhood trauma from having depression relapse.

Mindfulness meditation helps in regulating and controlling emotions. It also gives you the ability to step back from negative emotions and accept them, rather than what we usually do, which is to fight them. Fighting these negative emotions can lead to increased stress, anxiety, and eventually, depression. For these reasons, it is clear to see how Mindfulness meditation can help people cope with and manage their emotions and prevent depression.

6. Mindful meditation can help decrease loneliness, especially in elders;

Everybody feels lonely at times. It's not uncommon for someone to feel like they've been left out or forgotten by the people they love, and this can lead to someone feeling like they're alone in the world. This feeling is more common amongst elders, especially after experiencing the loss of a spouse. There is a study that showed reduced feelings of loneliness in elders after an eight-week long Mindfulness-based stress reduction program.

Benefits to Physical Health

1. Mindfulness can help manage chronic pain;

There are many people suffering from chronic pain, millions of people, in fact, and that number is rising every day. People are victims of accidents that leave them with disabilities and lingering medical conditions. Some suffer from post-traumatic stress syndrome, whether they are a survivor of a natural disaster or a vicious attack. Most people who suffer from chronic pain or post-traumatic stress syndrome are soldiers or veterans of the war that have come away with injuries they sustained during combat. Some people have been diagnosed with these problems due to other diseases like cancer.

Being able to manage chronic pain without the help of numerous medications and treatments is the main focus of many studies and modern research. The use of mindfulness-based stress reduction is commonly used in relation to chronic pain as it helps to relieve pain.

2. Mindfulness Meditation can improve sleep patterns and help with those restless nights;

The thing about not getting enough sleep one night is that the effects linger. Even if you think that you can catch up on sleep you've lost that is a much more difficult task than it sounds. This day-to-day life we live in requires more of us, and in order to meet our goals, whether it's for work or if it's personal, we end up sacrificing important things like our sleep. This can damage our overall health in multiple ways.

Getting a night of poor or little sleep is a domino effect, and the dominoes just keep piling up on each other until there's nothing you can do about it. However, mindfulness meditation can help combat these effects and let you get a good night's sleep. There is research which found an improvement in the quality of sleep in adults that practiced mindfulness meditation.

3. Mindfulness Meditation can improve your immune system;

The immune system is the bodies first and last defense against disease and foreign organisms that wish to do your body harm. Therefore, your immune system should be fit and healthy in order to protect your body from illness properly. In 2003 there was a study performed at the University of Wisconsin-Madison that showed an improvement in the functions of the immune system in people who practiced Mindfulness meditation.

4. Mindfulness Meditation can give you a healthy heart;

A healthy heart is the first step to a healthy body and a healthy life. One of the many things that cause a lot of harm to our hearts and our overall health is a compound called Lipid peroxide. This compound hardens the arteries in the heart, and having an increased amount of the compound can cause atherosclerosis. A health publication called Psychosomatic Medicine wrote about a study that proved people who practiced meditation had fewer amounts of lipid peroxide in their bodies. Other studies also show that mindfulness meditation can cause a person to have lower blood pressure, which also improves the hearts overall health.

5. Mindfulness Meditation can help you with your weight-loss goals;

Struggling with diets, exercise, and weight loss is something everyone has experienced. Mindfulness meditation has been proven in a clinical study done on several obese or overweight women to help manage weight loss more effectively. It did this in a way where it made the participants more mindful of how their emotions played a part in their weight gain by causing things like stress eating.

6. Mindfulness Meditation can lead to better overall health in women;

Most women of reproductive age suffer from a range of symptoms, especially leading up to and during their time of the month. The symptoms vary from increased fatigue, changes in appetite, irritability, anxiety, mood changes ranging from a slight increase in anger to full-blown depressive episodes. There was a study done by the University of North Carolina on women suffering these symptoms and other menstrual symptoms. The study showed that a woman who practiced mindfulness-based stress reduction had increased pain tolerance and could better control their emotions. It was also shown that these women were more aware of their bodies and accepting.

In this day and age, it is easy to learn about mindfulness meditation and take up the practice yourself. However, this means that the most difficult part of mindfulness is keeping up with the daily habit. You can only properly reap the benefits of mindfulness meditation when you stick to it and make it part of your life, not just treat it like a hobby.

There are a lot of different forms of Mindfulness Meditation, and each form gives its own benefits.

Benefits of Different Forms of Mindfulness
To understand mindfulness and the benefits, it can give you; it also helps to understand the different

forms of mindfulness and how each form provides its own kind of benefits.

Mindfulness meditation is not always straight forward and can be combined with other proven techniques to get results that you wouldn't normally see. These are called Mindfulness-based interventions and are often used by professionals as different forms of therapy. These Mindfulness-based interventions have been proven by several studies and numerous researches.

Medical forms of Mindfulness:

Mindfulness-based stress reduction is used worldwide to help participants with stress management and other stress and anxiety related issues. The Mindfulness-based stress reduction program was first founded in 1979 by Emeritus Professor of Medicine at the University of Massachusetts Medical Center, Jon Kabat-Zinn. Since its discovery, it has been the most successful program centered at stress reduction and management worldwide.

Some of the studies done had the participants record

the benefits they received from their experience with Mindfulness-based stress reduction;

11. Improvement in self-esteem

12. An increase in energy and enthusiasm

13. Greater coping abilities when it came to stress-related situations, short term, and long term.

14. An increase in the ability to relax

15. A decrease in physical pain

16. Greater ability to cope with pain

Mindfulness-based cognitive therapy was developed using previous research and study done by Jon Kabat-Zinn when he was developing Mindfulness-based stress reduction. Mindfulness-based cognitive therapy was further developed by Zindel Segal, John Teasdale, and Mark Williams more recently as the first clinical trial was only published in the year 2000.

This form of mindfulness is used to counter negative

feelings such as weariness, sluggishness, low mood incidents, and other such feelings that can lead to depression. Most people who suffer from an episode of depression are likely to continue a downward spiral and have a relapse. Mindfulness-based cognitive therapy has been proven to help people in these situations where they feel trapped by their negative moods.

Mindfulness helps people to realize when such negative moods are taking over, and they develop the ability to separate themselves from the negativity. After being given the ability to separate themselves from their thoughts and emotions, it becomes more clear to people that although those negative feelings exist, you don't have to let them overcome and control you. Mindfulness helped them see that the negative feelings and pain was a choice they could make, not a trap that left them helpless.

Further studies of Mindfulness-based cognitive therapy have brought to light the benefits participants were able to reap from the practice;

- Reduced chances of a depression relapse.

- The decrease in symptoms caused by depression.

- Lower levels of anxiety

- It helped patients manage their chronic pain and illnesses such as cancer, epilepsy, and diabetes.

- Decrease in stress

- Increased control over emotions

The mindfulness that can be done anywhere:

Mindfulness Meditation itself expands into many different forms, each one providing long-lasting benefits and making the overall experience more enjoyable.

Movement Meditation; this is usually used alongside other forms of exercise or relaxations such as yoga. During this meditation, you are aware of your bodily sensations, breathing, and your thoughts and emotions at the time. This meditation combines light exercise while practicing staying in the moment, so your body can properly relax and enjoy the activity.

Body Scan Meditation; this form of mindfulness is usually done while lying down, but any position that you feel comfortable in will work just as well. In this exercise, you will be able to become mindfully aware of your body and the sensations you're feeling. You will also be aware of how your mind often wonders to other ideas and thoughts. Although the idea of the meditation is to try and control yourself from doing this, you must not let yourself be overly critical when it does happen. This is a practice, and you won't be able to be fully mindful straight away.

Breathing Space Meditation; these sessions are usually short, and you'll only be mediation for about three minutes. You can do this more than once a day, and you should try and do it during stressful times or during a difficult situation. During this session, you should be mindfully aware of what you are experiencing, whether it is causing you a lot of stress or emotional pain. This idea is that being mindfully aware of such situations and experiences are better in the long run than trying to avoid. We are more likely to avoid uncomfortable situations, but it has been scientifically proven that being mindful of the situations is far more effective in the long run.

Expanding Awareness Meditation; this is usually done while sitting but can be done in any position that makes you comfortable. During this mediation, you are mindful of your body, and you should be focusing on your breath, body, sounds, thoughts, and feelings, usually in that order. At the end of the session, you should go into a state of open awareness.

Mindfulness of breath: Focus on your breathing, in and out. This is all you should do, focus on the in and out of your every breath. When your mind begins to wonder, and it will sometimes, make sure to bring your attention back to your breathing, but do not be critical or judgmental of yourself. Just focus on your breathing.

Mindfulness of body: Focus on every sensation in your body during each moment. You can do this alongside the mindfulness of breathing.

Mindfulness of Sounds: You must be aware of the sounds around you during your session, it will do you no good to drown them out or ignore them. Be aware of each ambient sound as it comes and goes and if there are no ambient sounds then instead, make yourself aware of the silence.

Mindfulness of thoughts: Being aware of your thoughts as each one surface in your mind and as they pass by. While you are aware of your thoughts, you must also be aware of distancing yourself from each one. You must allow the thoughts to come and go without lingering or attaching yourself to any of them. When you are mindful of your thoughts, you must allow them to be free, so you can also be free.

Mindfulness of feelings: You notice your feelings and emotions as you feel them, but you don't linger on them or let them control you. Feelings will arise during your session, and you should notice them and become aware of them. You should also accept them and let them pass if they want to rather than try to fight them or ignore them.

Open Awareness: this form of mindfulness is also called choiceless awareness. During this session, you should become mindful of whatever is predominant in your thoughts, so what you are more aware of. You do this without choosing what you are aware of. It is the most predominant thought in your mind at the time, and it could be something you didn't even know you were aware of until now.

There are other forms of Mindfulness Meditation. A most commonly used form includes visualization, such as imagining yourself in certain relaxing situations or places. Like a nice, calm lake, or an empty grass field. These kinds of meditations work on visualizing yourself in calming situations while maintaining your mindfulness of the present time as opposed to thinking about the past or worrying about the future.

Benefits of Mindfulness for Children, Teens, Young

adults, and Students

Mindfulness Meditation has become part of the hustle and bustle of modern society, and it has also become an essential part of the modern business man or woman's life. However, even though Mindfulness provides numerous benefits to those living in our busy world, it is not just meant for those working for a living. Mindfulness Meditation holds benefits for people of all ages, and the earliest it is introduced into a child's life the more they will be rewarded later on.

Benefits of Mindfulness Meditation for Children: Mindfulness can benefit our lives, from giving us inner calm to helping our self-confidence and ability to communicate effectively with those around us. Mindfulness can lead to healthy, meaningful relationships. When dealing with children, mindfulness lessens the effects of getting bullied, leads to reduced problems with attention, leads to an improved set of social skills, and improved mental wellness and overall health.

It's critical that educators and caregivers provide mindfulness practices appropriate for kids. This can be done by fostering mindfulness in kids through the use of objects, pictures, movement, music, and food. Using these tools help kids to develop their ability to focus at high levels. For instance, an activity where kids listened to songs while trying to feel a little sound on their belly going up and going down as they were breathing. Studies have shown that easy activities like the one mentioned have long-lasting and incredibly powerful developmental benefits if continually practiced.

Teaching mindfulness in school and at home will help to develop children and improve their mental health as adults.

Cognitive Benefits

Teaching mindfulness to young kids can dramatically influence their cognitive ability. Kids who were part of an 8-week mindfulness program showed major improvements in focus, behavioral regulation, and cognition compared to a control group of kids who didn't participate in the program.

Social Benefits

Social skills are any skills that a person uses to communicate and interact with people. Excesses and deficits in our social behavior can influence our ability to understand and learn. Kids who went through mindfulness programs were more compassionate and respectful of their classmates. Mindfulness teaches kids how to be aware of their feelings and bring compassion to their response to those emotions.

Emotional Benefits

Being emotionally healthy is important for successful adolescent development. Emotional issues like depression, stress, and anxiety can negatively influence a child's ability to perform, their self-esteem, and their social interaction with peers. Mindfulness has been shown to teach kids how to manage their anxiety and stress. It allows them to access their positive emotions and cultivate an enhanced sense of well-being and calm.

Mindfulness Meditation is simple but effective, and it will be easy enough for your child to get a hold of it no matter how young they are. The earlier they start, the better. The benefits of mindfulness for children are plenty:

1. Decreased risk of anxiety

2. Reduced amounts of stress

3. Teaches the ability to control and regulate emotions

4. Promotes optimism

5. Teaches organizational skills

6. Reduced amounts of aggression

7. Teaches good social skills

Mindfulness Meditation is also used in treating children with ADHD or other mental health issues. For these issues, however, a form of Mindfulness-based cognitive therapy is used, which is usually done by a trained therapist.

Benefits of Mindfulness Meditation for Teenagers: We all know that the world can be harsh, especially on young adolescents. There are lots of challenges and deadlines that make teenagers lives difficult in all sorts of ways. School is a battleground with social hierarchies, and although no one likes to think that their children won't be liked by other children, it does happen. Bullying is something that our children have to deal with every day, and they often keep it to themselves. There are other social issues that children face in school, one of them being peer pressure, and often our children are left to deal with these issues on their own.

Research done involving adolescents and children prove that there are some benefits to introducing them to Mindfulness Meditation. Some of the numerous benefits include:

- Improvement of sleep
- Reduced stress
- Reduced anxiety

- Reduced chances of depression

- Improvement in control over emotions

- Increased attention span and ability to concentrate

- Increased compassion and empathy towards other classmates

- Improved performance during tests and overall learning

Although Mindfulness Meditation has been proven to be full of benefits, it may be difficult to get a teenager actually to take it on willingly. In this case, you have to be willing to make the effort of sitting down with them and showing them all the rewards they can reap from a simple thing like meditation. If you are willing to take time out of your day, then they will be willing to listen to you and maybe even give it a try.

Your child's health is a fragile thing, especially at such a young age when they are not mentally equipped yet to handle it themselves. However, if you are trying to get your child to invest their time and effort into

Mindfulness Meditation, then don't be afraid to get in there and join in. You're probably already practicing it yourself, but your child might be more inclined to do it if you are willing to do it with them.

Meeting them halfway is the best option. Look at what grabs their attention and use that to steer them towards Mindfulness Meditation. Most teenagers these days are glued to their phones, laptops, computers, or any other device, and you can use these devices to get to them. There are plenty of apps your child can download on their device that can help them understand and learn Mindfulness Meditation. Once they get started and you put yourself out there to keep them on it, then they'll see how it's helping them firsthand.

So, take the step and show your child what Mindfulness can do for them.

Benefits of Mindfulness Meditation for Young Adults and Students:

Studying, part-time jobs, family, friends, moving out,

these are just some of the things that young adults and college students have to deal with. Their lives are a mess of deadlines, expectations, commitments, and responsibilities. It's all just a big juggling show, and everyone is waiting to see which ball they drop first.

The life of a college student or any young adult is filled with stress and anxiety, and they are more likely to fall into mood swings or drops that lead to depression. College students are more likely to fall into bad habits that can harm their health, one of them being substance abuse. In fact, college students have far more problems with alcohol abuse than the rest of the populations, and this can only lead to serious issues both academically now and for their future health and lifestyle.

There have been a few studies done on students in college as they are usually willing participants in such studies if incentives like extra money or academic credit are being offered. Studies like these have become more common, and they have found a lot more benefits for children being introduced to

Mindfulness Meditation at an early stage in their lives. The benefits range from helping them through their day to day lives as well as giving them the abilities they need to manage their academic and social responsibilities.

The benefits are listed below:

e) Increased curiosity

f) Increased tolerance

g) Decreased stress which affects overall health issues like substance abuse and mood swings leading to depression

The effect of mindfulness meditation on drinking in college students is believed to be due to the impact on their self-control. Students who participated in mindfulness-based stress reduction showed an enhancement in their self-control which led to fewer incidents of substance abuse

h) Better self-acceptance

i) Along with better self-control, they also experienced better self-regulation

j) Improved emotion regulation and decreased reactivity

k) Enhanced social skills and relational qualities

l) Provides better mental and emotional skills for dealing with bullying in and out of school

Although most of these benefits of mindfulness only affect the lives of young adults and college students, there are plenty more benefits for students of all ages. Not all children deal with the same difficulties like bullying or substance abuse, but mindfulness meditation has been proven to help with all issues no matter what age your child is or what issues they suffer from.

CHAPTER 3

Techniques to Practice Mindfulness Meditation

In this chapter, you will learn 10 different mindfulness meditation techniques that you can put into practice immediately. All the techniques explained are easy to follow and learn. However, mastering them will take time, patience, diligent efforts, and commitment. So, here goes:

Technique #1 –Mindfulness Meditation through Simple Breathing

This is, perhaps, the easiest technique to start off your mindfulness meditation journey. All you need to do is sit comfortably in a quiet place and identify your inhalation and exhalation. As you inhale, identify it as the in-breath and as you exhale, identify it as the out-breath.

Your mind is focusing on recognizing the in-breath

and out-breath as you breathe. That's all there is to this technique. You must focus your attention on the in-breath and the out-breath and recognize the inhalation and exhalation process as you breathe.

The nature of your mind is to wander, and so it will. Every time you notice that your mind is not focusing on your breaths and is instead wandering on other thoughts, bring it back to your breath and simply continue from where you stopped. Don't force yourself to do anything other than to observe and label your inhalation and exhalation.

Remember, the trick in this technique is to get your mind to focus on the breathing process, i.e., the inhalation and the exhalation. This technique is so simple that you can use it anytime you feel stressed out during the day.

For example, if you are having a difficult time with your boss or colleague and the stress levels are so great that you think your emotions are going to burst forth, quickly get away from the scene and find a quiet spot. You don't even need to sit down anywhere though the sitting position is ideal.

Otherwise, simply stand at one place and get your mind to focus on your breathing. When your mind's attention is taken off, even for a few minutes, from the stressful situation, there is an immense relief for it during which time it will recoup and regroup its thoughts and emotions. By doing this, you can act objectively and rationally.

Technique #2 –Mindfulness Meditation through Concentrated Breathing

The technique is an ancient and powerful one that has helped numerous practitioners achieve peace and contentment. In this technique, practitioners watch and observe their breath in a relaxed manner. The breath is used as an anchor for their minds to focus on. The difference between this and Technique #1 is that here you focus on the entire process, including movements and sensations that are part and parcel of the breathing action.

Sit in a comfortable position either on the floor or on a chair. Keep your back straight but not uncomfortably erect or stiff. Close your eyes, pay attention to your nostrils, and observe your breath. Focus on the sensations of breathing, which includes the following elements:

- Watch how the air enters your body through the nostrils

- Observe the feeling as the air goes down your throat and the windpipe into your lungs

- Feel the air released from the lungs come out through your nose

Don't force yourself to breathe in any particular way or speed. Don't try to control your breath. Breathe as you normally do. Only watch and observe the breathing process closely. Your mind will wander. You can't really stop it from wandering away to other thoughts. Every time, it moves away from the focus of breathing, be aware that your mind has moved away to other thoughts, and gently bring it back to the attention of your nostrils.

You can start with 15 minutes daily spread over three sessions of 5 minutes each. As you engage in this technique, you will find your own rhythm. Some people can sit for more than 5 minutes at a stretch. Some might find it difficult to sit even for this long, at least initially. Follow the technique and identify what suits you best. Slowly increase the duration of each session until you can do it for 30 minutes at a stretch.

There is another breathing method that you can use in this technique. It is called abdominal or diaphragmatic breathing. The ancient Hindu scriptures speak of the power that is held in the abdominal area. The navel chakra that is in the abdomen region is responsible for the efficient working of our nervous, respiratory, and musculoskeletal systems.

In fact, the ancient sages of the east only breathed through the abdomen. Breathing through the chest is considered a more modern invention driven by the need to do things fast. Here are the steps to follow for abdominal breathing:

- Sit comfortably on a chair or lie down on the floor. Place your right hand on the abdomen and your left hand on the chest.

- When you start breathing, notice which of your hands is moving more, and which direction it is moving.

- If the hand on your chest is moving in the upward and downward direction, then you are breathing through the chest only.

- In abdominal breathing, during inhalation, your right hand must move in the upward direction as the abdomen gets filled with air when you breathe in. During exhalation, your right hand must move in the downward direction as the air is being released out from the body. The left hand on the chest must move in the same way although to a much lower degree.

Focusing on these movements during diaphragmatic breathing can be another useful mindfulness meditation technique.

Technique #3 – Mindfulness Body Scan Meditation
This technique requires a more formal atmosphere than the breathing technique as it is best experienced when you are lying down or sitting in a really comfortable posture. While lying down may seem like a fabulous way, initially, it might not be a good idea in the long-run because novices tend to fall asleep in this position. Also, while a good 30-minute duration is needed for effective results, you may make the best use with whatever little time you get.

Sit down on a cushion or a chair or lie down comfortably on the floor. Avoid lying on a mattress if you find it difficult to stay awake. Close your eyes because it makes it easy to focus. Now, pay attention to your breath. Slowly move your attention to the places where your body is in contact with your chair or floor. Investigate each section of your body mentally.

The different sensations you experience could be tingling, pressure, tightness, temperature, or anything else. Sometimes, you may not feel any sensation too. Notice the absence of sensations also. Each section of your body becomes an anchor for your mind to hold on so that it doesn't wander away.

Again, be aware when your mind wanders, and gently get it back to where it was before it moved off. When you are done, open your eyes, and mindfully get your focus back on the outside environment.

Another crucial aspect of the body scan mindfulness technique is to release the tension in the various parts of your body as you scan it. When you focus on a particular section of the body, say your shoulders, you suddenly realize that you are holding them too rigid and creating tension in that area. By focusing on that part, tension is automatically released from there.

These are formal ways of body scans and breathing mindfulness meditation techniques. You can do these mindfulness activities even while sitting in your chair in your office. Take a 5-minute break and do a body scan or focus on your breath even as you sit at your desk. You don't even have to get up from your seat. Also, you could do it during your daily commute or while waiting for someone or standing in line for something or anywhere else. Mindfulness meditation does not need anything else but your mind, which is always with you.

Technique #4 – Mindfulness Meditation through Mantra Chanting

A mantra is a phrase, word, or syllable that is repeated during the meditation session. Mantras can be repeated in mind, whispered, or chanted aloud. Mantra meditation involves two elements, including the mantra that is being chanted and mindfulness meditation using the mantra as the anchor. Mantra chanting keeps the mind focused and facilitates mindfulness meditation. People also use the mantra as a form of positive affirmations.

Identify the best mantra for your needs. You can choose your mantra based on the reason for the mantra chanting. Are you looking at getting back your health? Are you seeking peace? Do you desire for something to happen in your life? Are you looking for a deep spiritual awakening?

Sit comfortably with your back straight but not rigidly erect. Focus on your breathing first, which will help you get into the mindfulness meditation state. Ensure your intention for the mantra chanting and meditation is clearly imbibed in your mind. Now, start chanting the mantra. Don't expect miracles when you start your chant. Simply repeat the mantra slowly, deliberately, and in a relaxed manner. In this mindfulness meditation technique, mantras are the anchors that help your mind to focus.

There are no 'best' mantras for mindfulness meditation. You can choose anything from the scriptures of your personal religion, or you can choose positive and empowering affirmations such as:

- I am happy and content at this moment

- All my treasures are inside of me

- My heart is my best guide

- It's always now

- I am complete, and I don't need anything outside of me to make me whole

- Nothing is permanent

- This too shall pass

Technique #5 – Mindfulness Meditation while Walking

Find a quiet and undisturbed place for your walk. While the outdoors would be ideal, even walking back and forth in a big hallway or your own small room will do for practicing mindfulness walking meditation.

Like breathing and body scan mindfulness meditation techniques, you can make walking a formal mindfulness activity or become mindful whenever you walk from any point A to any point B.

Walk at a naturally comfortable pace with your hands placed conveniently. You could keep your hands at your sides, on your stomach, or behind your back. For the initiates, counting steps from 1 to 10 and then back from 10 to 1 repeatedly helps in keeping the focus on the walking meditation. If you are walking in a closed space, then count the number of steps one way, pause intentionally and in a focused manner when you need to turn around and start counting again.

As you take each step, focus on the lifting and falling of your leg. Pay attention to the sensations in your legs and also on the rest of the body. Focus the way your body is shifting as you take steps from one leg to another. If your mind is captured by straying thoughts, be aware of this occurrence, and gently bring back your attention to the walking process and the related sensations and feelings. You must remember not to get frustrated as your mind repeatedly wanders. That is the nature of the human mind. Gently bring it back to the present moment.

When you are walking outdoors, widen the horizon of your awareness. Soak in everything you see, hear, and feel. Mindfulness walking in an outdoor environment keeps you safe too. Now, for a few minutes, focus on the sounds you hear. If you are indoors, then, perhaps, the whirring sound of the fan or the beep of the microwave oven or the sound of the television played in another room. Don't label any of the sounds you hear as pleasant or unpleasant. Only hear them as sounds.

If you are outdoors, then there are a lot more sounds you can hear; the chirping of the birds, the rustling of the leaves, the honking sound of vehicles, dogs barking, the movement of wheels on the road, or anything else. Try and recognize every sound that reaches your eyes.

Then, shift your attention to the smells around you, again without labeling them as good or bad. Don't compel yourself to recognize any smell or sound if it is difficult. Then, shift your attention to the things you can see; the colors, the shape, the objects, and more. If there are many elements, then focus on what comes to your attention and continue until the next one comes to your attention. But don't get entangled in the experience. Do everything at a natural pace without hurrying or slowing down needlessly. The trick here is to maintain sustained awareness of everything happening to you and around you.

Technique #6 – Mindfulness Meditation through an Empty Mind

This technique involves focusing the mind without any tangible anchor. Your thoughts are the anchors. Simply sit comfortably in a quiet place. Close your eyes and focus on the thoughts that are coming up in your mind. Don't react or respond to the thoughts. Let them float freely through your mind. Observe the thoughts as they enter and watch them leave. Don't be judgmental and don't get attached. Here are the steps to be followed for the traditional empty mind meditation technique:

- Sit in a straight-backed chair or on the floor with your back comfortably straight.

- Use abdominal breathing for this technique and watch your abdomen expand as you inhale and contract as you exhale

- Watch the breath entering your body through the nostrils and exiting through the mouth.

- Let your thoughts flow freely and observe each thought enter your mind, reach its peak, and fade away. Now, focus on the next thought and observe it until it fades away. Continue the same process for all the thoughts that come to your mind.

The trick here is to catch a gap between two thoughts when the mind is thoughtless for an instant. The moment is fleeting and extremely easy to miss. That is the ultimate aim of the empty mind technique. Until you achieve the level where you can catch the momentary thoughtless gap between two thoughts, merely follow your thoughts around wherever they go without reacting, responding, or being judgmental. This is the essence of mindfulness.

Technique #7 – Mindfulness Meditation through Observations

This technique is very simple and yet empowers you to appreciate and find joy in the little things around you in a very profound way. It is best done when you use something from nature for the observation technique. Not only will you find peace and happiness from the mindfulness meditation aspect but also from the beauty of nature that we so often miss in our stressed-out and rushed lives.

Choose a natural object from around you. It could be a small pretty flower or a nicely-shaped leaf or a little insect or the moon or clouds too. Keep everything else out of your attention except the chosen object. Watch and observe it in a relaxed way without putting any pressure to learn about it or label it. Observe it for as long as your concentration powers allow you to.

Remember to see the object as if you are seeing it for the first time, and notice every little element in it; the color, shape, smell, stand-out features, and more. Explore the entire object in complete depth and let yourself be consumed by it. Imagine energy waves from your body entering into the object and connecting with the energy waves of the object. This way, you will find that it is possible to see and feel connections with everything around, especially things in nature.

Technique #8 – Mindfulness Meditation for Increased Awareness

This technique helps you enhance your awareness skills and appreciate what you do even in the small mundane things of life, many of which you have taken for granted. Here is an example of such an activity.

You open doors every day, right? Do you really think about the act of opening the door? You simply take it for granted that when you turn the knob, the door will open. Mindfulness teaches you how to appreciate even this simple everyday task and convert it into a task of joy and happiness. Here's how:

The moment you touch the doorknob to open the door, pause for a little while and be mindful of how you are feeling and where you are. Focus on where you are standing and where this door will lead you. Then, touch the doorknob, and observe the way your hand turns which, in turn, results in the knob turning. Feel the inside elements of the knob revolving too.

Let your thoughts wander to those trees that were cut down to make this door. Think of the carpenter(s) who worked tirelessly to create and fix the door. If there is a glass pane on the window, focus on the process of how it was created and affixed to the door.

Pay attention to the hinges of the door and how they facilitate the action of the door opening. When you open the door, typically you would fill the rush of air. This might be very subtle when you are opening a door inside a house and more pronounced when you are opening the door to the outside. Notice this feeling too.

The same awareness goes for many routine activities of your life. When you start working on the computer, pause for a moment, and look at your hands and appreciate your ability to work on the device. Notice how your brain thinks when it comes to dealing with computers. It automatically behaves very differently from the way it behaves when it is dealing with people, right? Isn't that a magical moment of discovery?

Start this technique with one item each day, and slowly and steadily build it to about five items to observe and appreciate.

Technique #9 – Mindfulness Meditation in Conversations

In the modern world, rife with multiple distractions, having meaningful connections with people in your professional and personal life. Indulging in mindfulness conversations will help you develop such deep relationships. Here are some tips to follow a one-on-one mindfulness conversation:

Make sure all distracting elements such as your phone, tablets, computers, and all electronic devices that have notification sounds are turned off. Mindfulness in conversations is possible only when you are not tempted to give in to distractions.

Focus on the person's gestures to identify subtle and obvious body language cues which may be saying something quite contrary to the spoken word. Moreover, maintaining eye contact helps you see underlying emotions as well. If you do not pay attention to these elements, your conversation will lack authenticity and presence.

Focus on the speaker's tone of voice. Many people are trained to look happy even when things are going wrong. However, it is very difficult to keep your voice sounding happy, even when you are sad. Paying attention to the tone of the speaker's voice will give you a clue to his or her true state of mind. Showing your insightfulness during the conversation and gently talking about what's troubling the speaker will help you build trust and a deep connection with the person.

Pay attention to your own thoughts during the conversation. Ensure your mind is not carried away by thoughts that are not related to the current conversation. Each time, your mind wanders, gently bring its attention back to the discussion with your friend or colleague or loved one.

Focus on what the other person is saying without being judgmental. Even if the other person said something hurtful, don't react immediately. Focus on the words, and respond to the content and not the emotion in words. Dig deep and ask for the reason as to why the person said what he or she said. A conversation of mindfulness has to be without judgment and criticism necessarily.

For that matter, it would be great if you can avoid reacting overly to praise as well. Courtesy demands that you thank the person for the nice things he or she is saying. But, again, drag your mind's focus on what is being said and respond objectively to everything.

Choose to respond instead of reacting. The response happens when you think things through objectively and provide answers to questions posed. Responses typically do not have emotions. Reactions, on the other hand, are based on ungrounded emotions and are usually impulsive in nature. Responses rarely cause regret, whereas reactions invariably do so.

Pay attention to every word spoken by the other person and the feeling each of these words brings forth. Drown yourself in the emotion. However, don't react to them. Let the emotions course through your body and mind after which its power is bound to fade away. When this period passes, you will see that you can look at the information shared by the other person objectively using which you can handle the conversation maturely and purposefully.

As you increase your mindfulness and awareness during conversations, you will notice how evolved you become when it comes to handling difficult and unpleasant situations. Your ability to bring the focus of the conversation to a meaningful purpose will improve with each attempt. And this attitude will help you build sustaining positive relationships both in your professional and personal life.

Technique #10 – Mindfulness Meditation through Appreciation

Technique #8 was about mindfulness in enhancing awareness of the things and objects around us. The technique in this section talks about mindfulness meditation through appreciation and showing gratitude even for the seemingly small things in our life. There are so many elements that support and provide convenience to our lifestyle, and many of these things go unnoticed. Here's a sample list to consider.

- Your clothes keep you warm

- Your senses allow you to feel and enjoy the reality in which you exist

- The postman never misses delivering your mail

- Your home protects you from various natural elements

- Your oven and stove cook your food

- The fridge in your home preserves your food

- Focus on the following questions for each of the previous items and find answers to them:

- How did these things and processes come into existence? Who created them? Who thought of them first?

- Have you thought about how difficult your life would be if these items were not available to you?

- Have you thought about how dependent you have become on these things?

- Have you thought about how all these things are interrelated and how they play an interconnected role in the life of human beings?

When you focus on the answers to these questions, you will realize the wonderful miracles with each of the things that you have hitherto taken for granted filling you with joy and contentment. Moreover, an attitude of gratitude helps your mind to focus on the positive aspects of your life, helping you manage negativity easily and effectively.

The Importance of Following Mindfulness Meditation Techniques

The mindfulness techniques mentioned in this chapter helps in enhancing your moment-to-moment awareness levels. These techniques are all very useful in managing and controlling negative emotions and thoughts while reducing anxiety and stress levels in your life. You will not run on an autopilot mode anymore as you live each moment fully engaged with life. You will be able to develop a clear and free mindset and consequently be empowered to deal with all the problems and challenges that life throws at you with little or no difficulty.

Furthermore, with the consistent practice of these mindfulness techniques, you can leverage all the benefits explained in Chapter 2. Remember not to make mindfulness meditation something you do for a short period of time, and then forget about it. Instead, make it a way of life!

CHAPTER 4

Declutter Your Mind

Declutter your mind, or make room in your head, this is what this new way of saying means, that together with mindfulness is making space between the new lifestyles of Westerners like us, stressed and frantic.

If we feel completely unfocused, if we feel that our brain is becoming infinite chaos, it is time to make space, to do the cleaning and tidy up that box that is our mind. Like our closets and our storage rooms, the brain needs to be tidied up every sometimes, due to the continuous overcrowding of problems, thoughts, and concerns. To be productive, focused, and motivated, it needs to be stimulated and reset.

The disorder of our mind is the worst kind of confusion we can have in our life because it fills the brain and crowds it with useless things; this leads to difficulties in doing even the simplest things. Mental fatigue derives by both positive and negative

238 | Page

conditions of our life, but the latter does not allow oxygen to circulate in our mind, unlike the positive ones that stimulate hormones. It is as if our mind was a hard disk, once it is full we have to reset it, leaving only what is really necessary. A mind full of thoughts, untreated for a long time, can lead to the onset of diseases such as chronic depression and stress, which are linked to other chronic diseases for the body. Furthermore, this mental state can influence our social relationships because our energy will be exhausted, and it will not be enough to spend time with other people.

Decluttering, however, does not only refer to our mind, but it also refers to making space in our home, office, and in the places we frequent the most. Living in a cleaner and more ordered place keeps our brain calmer and more oxygenated, with much more new space for the beautiful things that happen to us in life. As we clear our minds, we should also clear our spaces full of thousands of junk.

So, let's try to find time to rearrange and decipher our

ideas, our thoughts, our home, our work environment. We are doing everything more easily, without stress.

To be able to rebalance the disorder in our mind, there are several suggestions we can follow, which will greatly space our heads.

6. Set ourselves priorities: "The problem of not having goals is that you can run up and down the playing field, but you will never get a score", said a famous poet, in fact, having priorities in life is a fantastic way to maintain always active the charge in our days and in our head. The first step to put this advice into practice is to understand what is most important to us, what our aspirations in life are and what our goals are. Having established this, we can draw up a list, the list of priorities to be put into practice. To have a list at hand, will motivate us every day to move forward and get us to organize an action plan to get where we want. This list, once we reach our objectives, even if not all, will have to evolve, as

we go on with years. Looking at it often will be a sort of alarm bell to awaken the mind towards our goals.

7. Let's write everything down in a diary: Writing in a diary is one of the best ways to relax our mind and organize the thoughts that pass through it. Expressive writing ejectsnegative thoughts, stimulates our memory and cognitive activities of our brain. Writing a diary page every day, telling us what happened to us, describing our emotions, is a healthy method to release positive feelings to ourselves and to the surrounding environment. There is no need to be verbose and write papyrus every day; even a simple outline is enough; the brain will respond positively to this.

8. Let go: accept ourselves, love each other, and go far. In doing so, we learn to release all emotions and negative thoughts that make us feel grounded. Eliminating the superfluous, the fears and what causes us stress, what makes us

feel in a cage, we would have a freer mind, with more space to fill with positive thoughts and emotions that make us happy and make us feel good. Regularly monitoring our thoughts and trying to replace unnecessary thoughts with positive thoughts is a way to live better and be more serene.

Negativity can be very demotivating and debilitating to the mind as it is heavy and takes up a lot of space. Sometimes negative emotions are needed, but these, in the long run, cause our body to become self-poisoned if we don't stop them. For this reason, we must learn to let go of everything that causes these negative emotions in us. The first step, in this case, is to understand first of all ourselves, how we talk, what we think and say. We must not be negative towards ourselves or towards others.

9. Avoid multitasking: even though it may seem counter-productive, doing a thousand things together only accumulates in us a lot of stress, tension, and makes our body and our brain

work twice as much. Research states that performing too many actions simultaneously lowers efficiency and damages the cognitive system. We must try to make a list of what we have to do during the day and focus on the most important things, without overdoing it, our body needs rest. We should try to write a simple and realistic list without exaggerating. Let's start with the most important things and conclude with the simplest and superfluous ones.

10. Breathe: stop sometimes, take air slowly, hold and then exhale. This action, done from time to time, will bring oxygen to the brain, deep breathing allows the blood to circulate better and to stimulate the parasympathetic nervous system that helps the body to relax.

11. Make space in our working environment: So, let's clean our office! Put away the superfluous things, throw away the objects we don't use, remove the dust, try to position the objects in

order, maybe in boxes to organize everything. Try also to maintain this cleanliness every day, of course, if we are exhausted we should leave it alone, but let us not abandon ourselves again to disorder. Working in a neat and clean environment makes it more productive and more efficient.

12. Be determined: if we constantly think about whether to make a decision or not, our brain space would be completely overwhelmed by thoughts and without oxygen. We would feel our heads burst. So quit mulling over things, let's be determined and go straight for that road. Regardless of the decision is to make a phone call, buy a new piece of furniture for the home, read an e-mail you've avoided for a long time. Start making decisions without thinking too much, without getting sick of an idea we have. This does not mean being superficial, not giving weight to things or anything else, it means not giving too much space to what

worries us for too long, not giving it a chance to ruin our days.

13. Share our thoughts: speak with our friends, with our partner or with someone who makes us feel comfortable, it's a great way to get rid of suppressed emotions. Sharing what worries us, trying to find solutions to our problems together with someone else will help us to feel better and make decisions more clearly.

14. Limit the use of the media: media, with which we are always in contact, have a big impact on our mental health. We are always online, reading blogs, news, chatting, making video calls, posting photos on social media. This information overload can clog up our brains, causing stress and anxiety. Limiting the use of media and information that we put into the brain, through media, will lead to make more space in our brains and to feel more active, because being in front of a monitor or a cell phone, however, does not help neurons.

Furthermore, the media often give us the bad news that influences our mood and our vital state.

15. Relax: let's take a break from time to time; the brain needs rest to recharge and not to become jelly. Turn off cell phones, computers, and engage in activities that makes us happy for a few hours a day, even a nap if we need it.

16. Spend some time into the wild: several studies have associated the importance of nature to the human mind and to pathologies that can affect it, such as anxiety and depression. Nature restores in different ways, refreshes and invigorates our mind and body.

When our mind is heavy, we should try to spend some time in the midst of nature, even if only for a few hours.

17. Do physical exercise: as we have already seen for yoga or for walking meditation, physical exercise helps our mind and makes us return

lucid. We must try to practice outdoor activities whenever possible; fresh air is much better than four walls.

18. Sleep a little more: sleep has many benefits, including to improve mental well-being. If we don't rest enough, we are sleepy, of course, but our brains are also lazy, and we don't want to do anything. Sleep deprivation interrupts the ability of brain cells to communicate with each other, forming tiny blackouts. Let's try to give more sleep to our cells, simply sleeping 8 to 10 hours a night and having a routine.

CHAPTER 5

Anxiety Mindfulness Meditation

Dealing with Your Day-to-Day Anxieties Writing
Prompt

1. How would you describe your current reality?
   How can you improve it?

2. How are you currently coping with your anxiety
   in your day-to-day life?

3. What can you do to rid yourself of the biggest
   trigger you are having?

4. What is one breathing technique you will do
   today to help deal with your anxiety?

5. What is one relaxation technique you will do
   today to help deal with your anxiety?

6. What one thing will you do today to make it a
   success?

Mindfulness Meditation Script For Anxiety #1
Collect your scrambled thoughts one by one. Put them

in a basket of forgetfulness. Tuck the basket away for the time being. Breathe in and breathe out while you collect your thoughts. Steadily slow your breaths down until you can only feel your body fill with the positive reassurance from every deep breath that you take.

Be still. Be calm. For the next 10 seconds, be completely at peace.

Look at the blank canvas of your mind. Think of situations that cause you anxiety. Do you see the vivid colors that are splashing on your mental canvas?

Feel your breath steady the white canvas. Exhale any thought and colors that may be coming to paint that canvas. Exhale and push them away until your mental canvas is totally blank.

Inhale slowly. Exhale slowly. Inhale forgiveness. Exhale anger.

You are the master of calm — the painter of calmness in your life. Breath slowly and deeply. Each breath steadies your mind's frantic thoughts. Keep the canvas as white as possible.

With every negative thought that wants to overcome your white canvas of calm, dump feelings of forgives and understanding and compassion and forgetfulness until the canvas is back white again.

Embrace the difficulty of trying to still your thoughts. Keep stilling your thoughts. When every thought of anxiety pops up, run your broad brush or love across it.

Feel the power of your breaths guiding your hands and helping you keep your brush steady and helping you paint with steady fingers and kind hearts and kind minds. Feel your body being reinforced by the positivity of your breaths empowering you to say all the right things that need to be said and to take all the right actions that need to be taken.

Do you see how white and bright your mental canvas is? Now splash kindness, understanding, gratitude, and love on the canvas. Keep your mental canvas with you. Know that you can return to this canvas to start over at any time.

Open your eyes and keep your mental picture with you.

Mindfulness Meditation For Anxiety #2
We will begin our mindfulness meditation for anxiety right now. If you are experiencing anxiety currently or have been experiencing it for a while, I know it is not the best feeling in the world. You may be hurting. You may be scared, but know that you're going to be okay. I know it is hard for you to believe this right now, but know that the responses your body is giving to your anxiety are going to be over soon.

Know that relief from your anxiety is coming. It does not last forever. You want to know why? It is because your body has a built-in stress relief already. Your body will naturally deal with anxiety on its own terms. So keep this gem in the back of your mind and know that your body is always helping you deal with your anxiety. It is up to you to activate the stress-relief by being relaxed. It is up to you to help your body relax by taking in deep breaths. The inhales are going to help calm your body. The purpose of this meditation is to use your breathing in order to relax.

You may feel like it is difficult to breathe, but be aware that your body is already breathing. Listen to your breath right now. If your breaths are short, try to lengthen your breath by breathing to the count of three. Breathe in for a cycle of three counts; 1, 2, 3. Then breathe out for a breath cycle of three: 1, 2, 3. Notice your heartbeat. Notice if it is going fast or slow.

Let's try to slow your breathing down. Breathe in again. This time we are going to hold the breath cycle for 5 counts. Breathe in 1,2,3,4,5. Then breathe out: 1,2,3,4,5.

Breathe in deeply again. Now breathe out like you're blowing a birthday cake with a lot of candles. You want to make sure that you are blowing each and every one of those candles out. Breathe in and hold your breath in for three counts: 1,2,3. Now breathe out slowly: 1,2,3. Keep this up. You're doing a great job.

For extra support, you can hold up your fingers and pretend they are the candles in front of you. Now blow the air out open your mouth and make a slight sound as you blow it out. Make a gentle 'hoo' sounds as you let your breath out. You can do this breath cycle one more time, or you can continue to breathe slowly and gently.

Be aware of your body. See how your body is controlling your breathing? Do you see how your body makes sure that it is getting enough air? Do you see how your body wants to help you calm down? In your comfortable position, close your eyes again and take it all in. Take in how awesome and self-sufficient your body is and how you can help it.

You may still feel overwhelmed. You may feel like no one is with you right now, but know that you are enough. You are breathing. Your breath is a wave. With every deep inhale you give, the higher the wave is. Ride the wave as high as you can. Breathe in and let your breath out with a big whoosh.

If you want to feel more comfortable, feel free to turn the light off or stand up and pace around as you continue with this breathing. If these steps do not help, know that your anxiety will continue to decrease on its own. You can continue to help your anxiety decrease by breathing. The more you breathe, the calmer you will be. Take it slow. Imagine with that feeling of calm feels like. Is it blue or yellow or white? Is it vivid, pastel, or bold? Feel that the deeper you breathe, the more you relax, and the faster your anxiety will go.

As you breathe, feel that is helping your body to relax. With each breath, you breathe in, breathe in deeply, and feel your body getting calmer. Please try and focus on your breath right now.

You do not have to worry about what is triggering you or causing you anxiety. You do not have to worry about what you're going to do to deal with the anxiety.

The only thing you should focus on is your breathing. Feel the flutter of the clothing against your chest every time you breathe in and breathe out. If you're feeling uncomfortable, and you need to find a more comfortable position, do so gently but continue to focus on your breath.

You are going to be okay. I know it doesn't feel like it, but you are going to be okay. Now we want to feel the warmth that's associated with calm. You can warm your hands together gently until you feel your palm slightly warming up. Do not go vigorously - go smoothly, slowly, and gently. Do you feel the warmth?

Now that you can focus on your hands moving, how does it sound? That sound can help you ground yourself from your anxiety and sent to you along with your breathing. When you feel that you focused on your hands enough, you can stop and place your hands by your side and breath in again.

Relax and know that anxiety is normal. Focus on the sensations of your body. Notice how they're different from when you first began. Listen to the sound your breath makes as you breathe in and you breathe out. Moment by moment, the breath is helping you pass this level of anxiety.

Anxiety is a natural process. It is not always easy to feel, but it is natural. Help your body react by continuing to breathe. Do not have any judgment about your state of mind right now. Know that life happens. But when you're able to be in this moment, just like now, with your breath, you can focus on the good. You can focus on just being. You do not have to make a decision to do anything. Just be here right now with your breath and your body. Know that you're going to be okay.

Accept your body for what it is. Accept your brain for what it gives you. Accept your responses for what they are because they are what they are. affirmations to help you and your body recover. You can either listen and continue to breathe slowly, or you can repeat them after with every breath.

Breathe in, and then breathe out. Repeat after me. "I accept who I am, no matter what I am feeling." The past does not determine who I am nor the future. The only thing that matters is the right now, and by accepting who you are now, you are mindful.

Breathe in, and then breathe out. Repeat after me. "I know that anxiety does not last forever. My anxiety will pass." Anxiety feels like it will last forever, but if you take it in the present moment, you will be able to ride the wave to calmness.

Breathe in, and then breathe out. Repeat after me. "My body is prepared to handle my anxiety. I can help by breathing." Be grateful and know that your body can handle any stress that it faces. The most important thing is to help your body out by breathing deeply.

Know that deep down inside, that as each second goes by, and as every minute goes by, I feel my anxiety going away. And I feel a large dose of calm replacing it.

Repeat after me. "I feel relaxed. I am more comfortable." As you continue to breathe, notice how the breath is affecting your body.

Breathe in, and then breathe out. Repeat after me. "I accept how I feel right now. I am calm. I'm going to be okay. I am relaxed. I am at peace." Keep breathing. You will continue to feel your body come down from the anxiety that you are experiencing. Pay careful attention to how your body feels in a relaxed state.

Great job. Notice how you feel. Continue to feel relaxed. Continue to breathe in and breathe out. Notice how lose your limbs feel. Notice how easy your breaths come and go. Notice how easy it is for your body to pick up on the next breath after you breathe one.

Continue to relax for as long as you want. You can continue to stay in your comfortable position and breathe in and breathe out, or you can go ahead and bring the meditation to an end. Whatever you feel like doing, be mindful of the decision.

On the count of three, this meditation will be ending. You can replay this guided meditation again if you need to or continue to breathe deeply and silently on your own. One. Two. Three.

CHAPTER 6

Meditation and stress reduction

What is Meditation?

Meditation simply refers to the mental state of thoughtless awareness. This essentially means you are actually meditating if you are aware of everything going on in your mind and around you without thinking or concentrating on that particular situation.

While it is hard to absorb everything going around and within us all the time (we have tens of thousands of internal and external stimuli every single day), in different cultures, numerous techniques are developed to guide people to reach this state of mental awareness.

If meditation is just a state of mind rather than an exercise that makes you think of something calming, then how does it help you to relieve your stress and anxiety? Let me explain:

How Meditation Helps Reduce Stress and Anxiety
As I stated above, meditation is a state of mental and physical awareness. This means that if you are in this state, then you can feel/experience everything that is going in your mind and your surroundings. Therefore, you feel or experience everything that is causing you to stress and making you anxious. As you are aware of yourself and surroundings, you detach yourself from the stress-triggering thoughts and circumstances and consequently get rid of the stress and anxiety.

Let me elaborate on that with an example.
Imagine you have been bullied throughout your whole life in school or by an elder brother or another family member. Since you have never received respect, you yearn for it and want everyone to love and respect you. Now you are at the stage of life where you have a job that you don't like and on top of that, a horrible boss. You are not getting respect at the office, and this stresses you. Think of this situation and try to imagine yourself in it. Then let's find out how you'd react to it: when you are mentally aware and when you aren't

mentally aware.

Case 1: You are not aware of your thoughts and surroundings. You don't know why your boss keeps shouting at you and why you feel stressed all the time. Therefore, you don't know what is it actually that you need to change in order to get your boss' respect. As a result, you just wing it; you keep repeating the same mistakes over and over again, which makes you lose respect the more with each passing day. Ultimately, you are likely to have greater levels of stress.

Case 2: You are aware of your thoughts and surroundings. You know that your mind is craving for respect. You are aware that your boss is shouting at you every day because he/she wants to see daily reports of the project he/she assigned you and you keep trying to avoid him because you are behind schedule. You feel the pressure of not meeting deadlines, and this makes you feel stressed, which in turn affects your productivity negatively.

Since you are aware of the situation and the reason

why you are stressed, you detach yourself from the situation through meditation and do your work without the fear of not beating the deadline. This increases your productivity and ultimately, you catch up with the schedule and start presenting daily reports to your boss. As a result, your boss starts respecting you again, as you are doing what he/she expects you to do and you are at peace as you are getting what you want: respect from others.

Basically, meditation increases your state of awareness and makes you conscious of things going around you, so you do what's important and discard the meaningless things from your life to become happy and content.

Well, you might easily assume that all this is simple logic, but the truth is that meditation has been proven scientifically to help combat stress, anxiety, and depression. Let me explain that before we start discussing how actually to meditate for stress and anxiety relief:

In one study, participants who meditated were noticed to have a greater ability to handle various stressful multitasking tasks as compared to those who never meditated. Meditation does this by initiating different changes in your brain. For instance, whenever you meditate, your frontal lobe (part of the brain involved in reasoning, planning, emotional control, and self-conscious awareness) tends to go offline, which essentially means you are less critical of yourself.

That's not all; meditation can lower the flow of data into your thalamus, thus resulting in reduced alertness, which means you are less responsive to external stimuli. Moreover, through meditation, you can increase your focus on creating as well as strengthening such virtues as compassion. To add on, some types of meditation help reduce the density of grey matter in the areas of the brain that are responsible for stress and anxiety, which in turn means you are likely to be less responsive to stress and anxiety triggers.

The thing is; through meditation, you can notice increased focus and greater ability to ignore distractions. To prove that, scientists collected data using functional magnetic resonance imaging (fMRI) and the results were astonishing; those who meditated noticed a relaxed default mode network. To help you to understand the concept of fMRI, we will briefly talk about the brain regions that are activated when you are at rest/relaxed because this is often associated with reduced anxiety and improved focus. When you meditate, you increase alpha rhythms, which are often connected to creativity, learning, relaxation, and great focus. The brain uses many neurons, which usually uses electrical energy to communicate with each other and ultimately create a pretty harmonized network that is linked to a certain state of consciousness. It is through the synchronized electrical connection that brain waves come into existence; such medical equipment like an electroencephalogram (EEG) measures these brainwaves.

The brainwaves exist in different frequencies (5 to be

specific), i.e., alpha, beta, delta, theta, and gamma, and these affect you in various ways. For instance, if you are fully alert and awake, the active brainwave is beta. This helps you to direct your attention to problem-solving and decision making. Well, the problem with this statement is staying in this state for too long is bad for you because it can cause stress and anxiety given that often, logic and critical reasoning can trigger an endless stream of negative thinking pattern, which could even cause mental disorders.

Of the 5 brainwaves, the most useful one for relaxation and treating stress, depression, and anxiety is the alpha brainwave. And the good news is that meditation can easily help you to get to this brainwave such that you lower sensory inputs and clear your mind of unwanted thoughts. In simple terms, the alpha brainwaves can help you to focus on one specific thought as opposed to having an endless stream of thoughts. In this state, your brain has increased awareness along with greater focus, which means your mind is likely to focus on certain stimulus for a certain duration of time and as a result, this can help you to apply various positive feelings, which can help you to overcome negative thoughts.

Now that you have learnt how meditation can help you reduce your stress and anxiety levels (by getting you in the alpha brainwave) let's move on and learn some of the techniques to perform meditation.

CHAPTER 7

Benefits of Meditation

You cannot achieve what you want in life when you cannot think clearly, if you feel stressed, have trouble focusing on your work and are victimized by health and psychological problems. In addition, you cannot get to your goals when you lack creativity, keep worrying about your past, are forgetful of the present, do not feel connected to yourself or others, are addicted to unhealthy practices and have no control over your thoughts, emotions, and feelings.

Lucky for you, meditation can help you gain freedom from all these by doing the following:

1: Reduces Stress

There are countless studies that show how mindfulness-based meditative techniques can significantly reduce your stress levels when practiced consistently. This is mainly because meditation reduces the denseness of the brain tissue that has been linked to worrying, which in turn reduces your anxiety and stress.

Moreover, meditation regulates the production of the hormones associated with stress and depression such as cortisol and adrenaline, and those associated with happiness and emotional stability such as dopamine and serotonin. When these hormones stabilize, you feel stressed only when you ought to and not at all times, and are able to feel emotionally and mentally stable and happy.

Naturally, when you can combat stress effectively, your focus at work and other areas in life improve. This can greatly help you to achieve your goals.

2: Can Improve Your Sense of Wellbeing
A chaotic state of mind can keep you from doing what you want and feeling good about yourself. You may wish to engage in a healthy habit, but your racing mind may never allow you to do so.

Meditation can help you calm down the racing mind to allow you to unwind, do what you wish to and enjoy a sense of wellbeing and contentment. By so doing, this improves your self-esteem, self-confidence and turns you into a go-getter.

3: Can Improve Your Sense of Empathy, Connectedness, and Relationships

More precisely, by practicing loving-kindness meditation, you rewire your brain to focus on positivity and unlock your empathy. When your sense of empathy and connectedness improves, you are able to bond better with people. This can greatly improve your relationships, love life, and happiness levels.

4: Can Improve Your Focus

Various studies show how meditation can improve your cognitive abilities, including your memory and ability to process and recall information, consequently improving your focus. Excellent focus is exactly what you need to avoid distractions, concentrate on high priority tasks, and perform to your optimal level to maximize your productivity. When your productivity increases, you are able to achieve your set targets better, which in turn helps you to manifest your desires and live your ideal life.

5: Can Unlock Your Creative Side

Studies also show that meditation can help unlock your creative abilities by strengthening the right side of your brain, which is associated with innovation, creative thinking, and imagination. When the right side of your brain functions optimally, you are better able to think outside the box, come up with intuitive solutions to annoying issues, and tap into your imaginative side. This can help you resolve the many challenges you experience in everyday life as well as find smarter ways to reach your goals in less time.

6: Can Help You Overcome Addictions

Meditation can give you better control of your thoughts by becoming more aware of them. This awareness can, in turn, help you understand your addictions along with their triggers and manage them effectively to break bad habits slowly.

7: Can Improve Your Decision Making Skills

When your focus and the ability to think rationally

improves through meditation, your decision-making skills naturally improve. In addition, studies show meditation can strengthen the part of your brain involved with decision making; thus, improving your decision-making ability.

8: Can Strengthen Your Heart and Improve Your Health

Studies show meditation improves cardiovascular health, reduces chances of having high blood pressure and diabetes, and stabilizes the conditions if you are already experiencing them. It also helps cure joint and muscular pains, provides relief from arthritis, improves immunity to the common cold, and helps battle viruses and infections better.

Meditation does have the power to change everything in your life for the very best, and if you just give it a try and then push yourself to be consistent with the practice, you will forever be indebted to yourself for making that decision.

CHAPTER 8

How Meditation Works

The aim of meditation is to create a balance of the mind, the emotions, and the physical body.

For centuries, the Eastern world has known and reaped the benefits of meditation. Finally, in the last century, the Western world has not only caught on to this practice, but it has also actively studied why and how it works.

It has been proven many times that mental stress is both the trigger and cause of many of the physical ailments we suffer. In order to begin to gain some control over our physical health, we must first gain some control over our mental health.

Meditation is increasingly being used to treat anxiety, depression, and stress. This is having a knock-on effect on our physical bodies, and helping with issues such as chronic pain, heart problems, digestive issues, blood pressure, memory and concentration problems, and an improved immune system.

It has even been used effectively in helping with the treatment of addictions to nicotine, drugs, and alcohol.

But how can sitting quietly for 15 – 30 minutes a day, achieve all this?

AND

Can we gain benefits from when we first start to meditate, or will we have to practice for months before we notice any improvements?

Meditation allows us to calm our mind and take it away from everyday life. It harnesses our prana, (life energy) and focuses it internally, allowing it to flow uninterrupted through our Chakra's.

Dr. Ron Alexander, Psychotherapist, Director of The Open Mind Training Institute in California and Author of Wise Mind Open Mind, states that the brain has five categories of brain activity.

The Gamma State:

Gamma is when the brain is very active and able to absorb information. It is a level of hyperactivity which, if given too much stimulation, will cause feelings of anxiety.

The Beta State:

This is the most common state of mind. It is the thinking state which allows us to plan, work, analyze, and problem solve.

The Alpha State:

The is the relaxed state where we are able to enjoy the moment, take pleasure in things around us, feel pleasure, and experience a calm state of awareness.

The Theta State:

The state we enter when we meditate. This is where our conscious mind switches off and is replaced by our unconscious mind. It is a place where we are free from the external interferences of everyday life and the doctrines of society. We are aware of surroundings but are tuned in to our deeper selves, at one with energies of nature. In Theta state, we are able to access our intuition and become more aware of our true being.

The Delta State:

For most of us, this is a state reached only during our deepest sleep state. People who have dedicated their lives to meditation, such as the Buddhist Monks, have the ability to reach this state at will.

The Sympathetic Nervous System is the cause of our Fight or Flight response. It is responsible for the turmoil within our minds. Dr. Herbert Benson, the Mind & Body medicine Professor at Harvard Medical School, has carried out a number of experiments on meditation. His findings show that while we are in a meditative state, our blood flow is re-directed to the parasympathetic nervous system instead of the sympathetic nervous system.

This causes a state of relaxation, slows our heart rate,

and causes the body to require less oxygen. In addition to the higher levels of awareness this achieves, the physical and mental benefits we gain from daily meditative practice are huge.

Daily practice will stop your stress levels from reaching a point which will cause illness. The long term benefits won't be achieved instantly. Like anything worth having, you will need to work at reaching the Theta state.

In the beginning, you may find yourself easily distracted, but regular practice will improve your focus. Your mind needs to be trained, and the more you practice, the easier it will become until you reach a point where you barely need to think about it.

It is unlikely you will notice much benefit in the beginning, as you are learning to achieve a meditative state, but within a few weeks of daily meditation, you should be starting to recognize the difference in your physical and mental wellbeing.

Over time, this will continue to improve as you

become better acquainted with your inner self, and any physical discord your body may experience.

The benefits of daily meditation over the first few months should include:

A more relaxed state

Better quality of sleep

Ease of stress and a lessening of muscle tension

Increase in energy levels

Increased stamina

Some areas of the body may experience a lessening of pain

A clearer, more focused mind

Better awareness of self

The outlook is more optimistic

A general feeling of calm

Increase in patients with others

The long term benefits of daily meditation should include:

Improvements in overall health

Improved immune system leading to less illness and a quicker Recovery from illness

Circulation is improved

Pain   is   reduced

Improved social skills

Self-motivation is high

Memory and thought processes become stronger

Confidence Increases

Deep recognition and understanding of your true self and the world around you

Strength of mind

CHAPTER 9

Different Kinds of Meditation

The reason that I have added this chapter is that there are different kinds of mindfulness meditation that can help you to realize your goals, and some may be better suited to you than others. If you find, for example, that you have difficulty using the counting of the breath because thoughts keep invading, perhaps Chanting Meditation will help you, because it focuses the mind on the chant that you are usually given by your Guru. For the sake of clarity, a chant or mantra is simply a group of words that are repeated and that may not actually have any meaning to you. That's not the point of the mantra. The mantra is to help ground you into the moment so that your thoughts are less likely to wander and you find yourself working with your breath as you meditate.

Chanting Meditation
The Om chant is the easiest one to remember because

it is what is used for meditation in general when you do it via a yoga class. Om is simply a word that you chant on the outward breath, but it takes a little while to get used to chanting. You may want to do this privately, so make sure that the space you have for meditation gives you the privacy that you need. It's not the sound depth that counts; it's the fact that the chant goes with the outward breath and is chanted through lips that are a little apart so that there is a kind of tingle to your lips as the chant is sung. The pitch that you choose for the chant is also something that you can determine based upon what's comfortable to you. Not everyone can chant in a high voice, but it should be the natural sound that comes from you when you simply hum something.

Using the Om chant, get into position as with previous instructions and when you are ready to meditate, breathe into the count of 8 and out to the count of ten until you get that rhythm going with your breathing so that you no longer have to think about the length of your breath. Now breathe in again and on the out breath, chant the word Om, to the count of ten. Breathe in again to the count of eight, and chant to the count of ten. You can easily pick up the numbers in your mind, and this method of meditation is particularly helpful for people who find it very hard to drop their thoughts while meditating. The concentration on the chant and the breathing will be enough to keep your mind occupied while you meditate and again if thoughts do come to your mind, you simply see them as passing friends and wave them goodbye in your mind because now is not the time to share your life with them.

It is a great way to meditate as your awareness is always on your breathing or your mantra and your mantra may not even mean anything to you which means that you are not picking up thoughts from it. There are several mantras that you can use, but, as a beginner, I would suggest the Om because it's the easiest one to remember. Here are some others that are relatively simple to retain in mind and more advanced meditators may enjoy using these.

So Hum is an easy mantra to remember, and it was originally written in Sanskrit and means I am. That's a really simple mantra and may help those who want to find an alternative to Om.

Sat Nam – This means literally that truth is my name. The idea with this mantra is to extend the Sat until it is about 30 times longer than the Nam part of the mantra. It may take a little practice, but it will be worth it because it is something that you can use while meditating or independently of meditating.

NetiNeti – This is a mantra not to be used when you are meditating, but when you want to expel thoughts from your mind that are negatively impacting your life.

While chanting while you are meditating can be helpful, you must remember that chants have other purposes and can help you to dispel negative thought patterns from your mind. When you find in your everyday life that you are chased by negative thoughts, you can merely replace them with a mantra that is sung silently to yourself, particularly the netineti mantra that is intended for expelling thoughts of this nature.

If you do chanting meditation with a Guru, you will usually be given a mantra that is meant specifically for you and is based upon your time and place or birth or Vedic astrology. However, when you are taking up meditation on your own, the above mantras will suit everyday use to try to concentrate the mind on the moment, rather than on any kind of thought pattern.

Mindfulness Meditation
This can be done in different ways depending upon your needs. For example, you can use mindful meditation to make you aware of your breath as is taught by major yoga classes, or you can choose something specific to focus on while you are meditating, such as the movements of the body as you breathe or the feelings that come from inside you. In either case, the pose for the meditation is the same as given in the chapter on meditation, and you are encouraged to let go of worldly thoughts and place all

of your attention on your breath. If you find that your mind is wandering, you can feel the changes in your body as you breathe, for example, the rising of the upper abdomen as the air goes into the body and the lowering of this area as the air goes out of your body. You may even notice changes in your temperature or changes within the position of your shoulders while you breathe and focusing on the breath is the whole point of this exercise. There is another form of mindfulness meditation that you can try before you take up meditation on a daily basis, and this will help you to become aware of the moment.

In this case, sit somewhere where you will be peaceful and place your feet flat on the floor, just as you would when you meditate. Now start to breathe in through the nostrils to the count of 8 and out to the count of ten, but this time keep your eyes open. This kind of meditation can be done at any time during your day, and a natural environment will encourage the breathing in of fresh air and the feeling of energy. While you are breathing observe your thoughts and as a thought comes to your mind, let go of it and replace it with something that your senses pick up like an aroma or a color, a touch or a sound that is inspiring. Do not make anything of this thought. Simply be in the moment and awaken your senses. When thoughts come to your mind that is unfitting to your meditation, simply let them go and imagine them flying away like leaves from an autumn tree.

This kind of meditation is useful when you have time on your lunch break or when you simply need to energize before a meeting. It's something that you can do with your eyes open, but it's best to start this kind of meditation in an environment that is calm, and that does not produce too many distractions. Remember you are celebrating the moment and breathing it in, with all its variances and allowing your senses to pick up on the beauty of that moment.

Focused Meditation
This form of meditation is where you have a purposeful focus for your mind. You may use a candle or perhaps an inspirational image, but during the

meditation, you focus your mind and your eyes upon this image and nothing else. This can also be done with a recording that is specifically made to help you with your meditation. This may be musical or have music in the background, but it will never be loud or something that will take your attention to the actual process of meditation. It is simply something to give your mind a focus. The point is that even if you were to concentrate on a pebble during the course of this type of meditation, you would see that with each moment passing it changes, and you are simply to keep your focus on that object while you breathe in and out in the same way as you do with other meditation systems. In Buddhist temples, you will often find a Buddha statue, but you may also notice that there are colored areas, which use pale pastels, and these could be of flowers or lotuses, but the point is that they provide something of inspirational value to those who are trying to meditate.

Sit in your normal meditation position and as usual, start to breathe in through the nostrils to the count of eight and then out to the count of ten. Keep doing this until your breathing is regular and you know that you can keep to that rhythm even without counting. Then focus your eyes onto the object that you have chosen, or alternatively your ears onto the sounds you have chosen. In the case of the latter, you can keep your eyes closed and simply let yourself be absorbed by the music as you breathe. The continuation of meditation takes about 20 minutes when you are accustomed to meditating in this fashion, and this may suit those who find that thoughts wander in and out of their minds easily or who are easily distracted from the purpose of meditation. If a thought enters your head that is not related to the meditation, then remember to let go of it and take your mind back to the focus of your meditation. It is not wrong that you have these thoughts. Your mind is not accustomed to stillness, and it will take a while before it gets accustomed to it. Some people even create a special space for this kind of meditation where they are inspired perhaps by the light or air within that room, and it's a good idea to choose a place that fills you with inspiration.

Walking meditation

This kind of meditation is useful for you in your everyday life. There may be times of the day when you feel too stressed or when you need to ground yourself so that you are able to concentrate on what lies ahead. For example, if you have exams to take, or if you are going for an interview and want to appear calm and collected, then walking meditation may help you to do that. Choose a place where there is not too much distraction at all. The idea is that you walk in reasonable circles and while you do so, you look down at your feet and are guided into observing the movement of the limbs and the rhythm of the breathing. For this type of meditation, I would suggest that you breathe into the count of seven and out to the count of eight. You certainly don't want to be so relaxed that you cannot stand up! As you breathe in, feel the rhythm of the breath as you lift your leg from the floor. As you breathe out, feel the rhythm as your foot touches the floor, and you make ready to move the other foot. Breathe in, and move the second foot from the floor and be aware of all of the movement of muscles within your leg as you move forward placing your foot onto the ground with the exhale.

You may wonder what good this will do. The reason that you need to learn to breathe in harmony with the movements of your body is that this allows you to be more aware of self and less aware of all of the problems that surround your life. You are grounded into this moment in time, and as you follow your path and continue breathing and observing in this way, you are effectively meditating at the same time — however, a word of warning. You will need to look in a downward direction so that you do not misplace your foot. That's perfectly acceptable. The best kind of surface for this kind of meditation is a flat surface because you don't have the additional worry about stumbling and falling and don't have to pay attention to external things like the slope of the ground. It's all about internalizing and being in the moment as you move forward and breathe with the motion of the body.

Meditation in the workplace and while traveling
You may feel that it would be impossible to meditate while you are working or when you are traveling, but you would be wrong. Many people who practice mindfulness enjoy the benefits of meditation during the course of their working or traveling time. Have you ever been in an airport and had time on your hands between flights? The chances are that you have and that you may have indulged in people watching or even eating simply to pass the time. That's why airports have loads of distractions such as shops and restaurants because they know that the people who pass through airports have time on their hands and may as well be spending money. However, there's nothing to stop you finding a quiet place and using this time to find clarity or peace of mind. Travel can be stressful, and even when you are on a plane, you may find that mindfulness and meditation can help you to pass the time in a productive way.

When you first learn meditation, you tend to cut out all of the potential distractions, but as you get more and more experienced with meditation, you can use it in any environment, simply to distance yourself from the noise around you and breathe and be in the moment. So how does this work in a travel environment?

As long as your luggage is safely placed beside you and you are not worried about things, there's nothing to stop you from meditating and using the breath to be in the moment. You don't even have to close your eyes. In fact, being aware of movement around you in a situation such as this is probably a good thing.

However, try to find something to focus on so that you are not disturbed by all of the movement and sounds around you. This focal point helps you to keep your mind on your breathing control, and this can be done even when you are in a busy environment. Breathe in through the nostrils to the count of eight, feeling the air entering your lungs. Then, breathe out to the count of ten, feeling the air leaving your lungs and finding its way out of your body as I told you at the beginning of this journey. It's not about concentration. It's merely about being. You can be anywhere at any time, and that includes in a travel situation or even in your work situation.

Walking meditation is a useful kind of meditation for the workplace. In the case of this situation, you can use it to clear the mind. Even if you can't go outside in the park or a place that is similar, there's nothing to stop you using the corridor at work and breathing in time with the movement of your foot from the floor and exhaling as your foot touches the floor. Being in the moment simply means letting go of all of the thoughts and simply breathing. Thus meditation is something that can be done even in a busy workplace, simply by breathing in the correct way, with the correct posture and allowing yourself that silence of thought. Sometimes, you can use this to distance yourself from negativity as well. If you find yourself in a confrontational situation, it may be better to excuse yourself and to distance yourself from it and go somewhere private to meditate for a short while. It's not irresponsible to do that. In fact, after you have meditated for a while, you are better geared up to dealing with a negative situation in a positive manner. Meditation clears your mind and reminds you of the importance of non-judgmental response.

Keeping up the motivation

I told you that in the early days it would be difficult at times and you may even feel like giving up, but I also put you through your paces with breathing exercises and exercises to help you to feel humble because the humble response to your obligations is a very wise one. Humility tells you that it's not you that is important, but the mindfulness that you put into your everyday life. I also explained about how the mind retains habits, and at the end of the day when meditation is retained as a habit, you will find that it takes very little effort at all and will one day finish your meditation and wonder about getting up and starting it. I know that this has happened to me and it has happened to several of people when you get the switchover from meditating purposely and actually doing it as a habit. It's a wonderfully eye-opening experience if you can keep it up and if you need to motivate yourself, there is nothing wrong with keeping an optimism journal where you write all the things that you are grateful for in your life and to refer to this each morning. You may even find inspirational quotations on the theme of meditation on your smartphone and can use this to guide you toward improving your life and carrying out your meditation, even on days when you don't really feel like it.

Some people have asked me how you know whether you are doing it right. The fact is that you are doing it. You are becoming more present in your life, and regardless of the fact that thoughts keep coming into your head, meditation is helping you. You learn to let go. You learn to be present in your life, and by doing so, the way that you respond to others will change as well as the way that you view your place in the world. You can't pinpoint an exact day when it all went right. It is just part of the process. Just as you would not question whether you are breathing correctly because you are still alive. You don't need to questionability –

as it's not ability related. You don't need to question whether you are doing things the right way – as long as you follow the instructions, wear the right clothing and keep your back straight, you are bound to be doing it right. If it takes a little while for you to feel that you are benefiting from your meditation, perhaps you are laying too much judgment on your own actions, and that means spending a little more time in mindfulness and becoming aware of what makes you judge so that you can take judgement out of the picture. Motivate yourself for the first month to six weeks and meditation will come as naturally to you as cleaning your teeth or taking that first call of nature in the morning. All of the while that you are doing this, you are clarifying who you are and your part in life.

Meditation helps you to do that, to make decisions, to feel good about your life, so there is no question that it will help you, even if you don't see a huge difference in the first couple of weeks.

CHAPTER 10

How to prepare for meditation

We've seen various kinds of meditation and now it is important to share some basic guidelines on how to properly prepare yourself for meditation. There is no hard and fast rule on what to do and not do or what to wear or not.

However, there are certain do's and don'ts, which if you take care of will enhance your overall meditative experience and help you settle into this new practice comfortably. Let's begin.

Pick a Nice Spot

On average, we have somewhere between 50,000 to 70,000 thoughts daily. Put into perspective, that's roughly 2083-2916 thoughts per hour or 35-48 different thoughts per minute! This means that we are never really focusing on one thing. The thing is; we tend to have more thoughts when surrounded by clutter or scores of things that remind us of more activities, chores, and thoughts. Therefore, if you meditate in any such place, you are likely to feel distracted several times during the practice.

A good fix to the problem is to pick a nice, calm spot, preferably one with only a few items, as this will be less distracting. As such, you will be able to meditate easily in such an environment.

It is advisable to choose a clean, organized nook or room of your house and dedicate it entirely to meditation. You can place any object that calms you down there or lights a few scented candles to soothe your senses; for some people, a small miniature figurine of Buddha does the trick. You obviously have the liberty to pick whatever you want or opt for nothing at all.

When you dedicate a place entirely to meditation and meditate there regularly, it soon turns into your meditation trigger. This means that every time you sit in that spot, you easily enter a deep state of reflection and start to meditate.

However, this does not imply you must always meditate in the same spot. You can meditate in a park, garden, in your car, kitchen and absolutely anywhere you want. For starters, it is best to choose a nice, clean spot, and once you build enough focus, you can then easily meditate anywhere you like.

Choose a Time of the Day You're Free

Meditation is extremely important for you, but in the start, when you do it, you will find your thoughts wandering off to scores of other tasks. This distraction can ruin your focus and interest in the practice, which is why it is advised to meditate during a time of the day when you are free, even if it is just for 5 to 10 minutes. When you know you have nothing else to do, you will find yourself focusing better on the practice.

Wear Comfortable Clothes

While you can buy comfortable yoga pants and shirts to get started if you are cash strapped, wear any clothes you have that you feel super comfortable in because you definitely do not want to be tugging at ill-fitted pants and feel annoyed during the practice.

Keep a Timer

If you have a timer or can get one, do so as it helps you set your meditation time, and in so doing, you will not have to check your phone for it constantly. For some people, even a 5-minute long meditation session tends to feel a bit annoying, boring, or overwhelming, mainly because they just don't know how to focus on one thing at a time. This makes them check the time frequently in hopes of getting done with the session quickly. With a timer, things become more convenient because you know it will beep once the time lapses.

Get a Zafu

A zafu is a round cushion designed particularly for meditation. You sit on it to give your hips and lower back enough support during the practice and avoid back problems. As such, it is best to invest in a good quality zafu to give yourself the necessary support when you sit to meditate.

That said, it is not compulsory as some people do just fine without it as well. You can use a regular cushion, pillow, or even a folded blanket to support your back and hips when you meditate if you don't feel like spending a few dollars on a zafu.

Comfortable Pose

You can meditate while taking any of the following poses but then again, it is your choice entirely. If none of these poses suits you, or you feel they are too advanced for you, simply sit on an exercise mat or rug on the floor, or plop on a couch or chair, or just lie down on your bed. Lying down to meditate is often not advised, as it makes a lot of people drift off to sleep. However, if you are tired, but want to meditate, lie down.

1: Full Lotus Pose

You sit with your legs crossed and both feet resting right on the top of the opposite thigh. It is the most symmetrical pose and helps you achieve great balance in your body.

However, since it is slightly difficult than its other two variations, beginners often avoid it in the start.

2: Quarter Lotus

It is an easy variation of the full lotus pose wherein you sit comfortably with both legs crossed loosely and your feet resting right below the opposite knee or thigh. For beginners, it is an easy pose to execute.

3: Half Lotus Pose

In this pose, you keep your legs crossed and rest one foot on the thigh opposite to it. You can fold the other foot underneath your top leg.

4: Burmese Pose

If crossing your legs feels uncomfortable, sit with both your feet plopped on the floor as shown in the image below.

5: Seiza Pose

This is a relatively easier pose than the crossed legged ones, as you simply kneel on the floor and then prop up on your legs as shown below.

Sit in a Chair

If none of these poses work, take a chair and simply sit on it with your back straight, while ensuring to maintain the small curve in your lower back while planting your feet firmly on the ground.

Pick any of these poses or lie flat on your back on the floor or your bed to meditate. Remember to listen to your body and do what feels right at the moment. With time and practice, you will get better and will find the strength and courage to try new poses.

Peace

Meditation can definitely help you achieve your peace of mind, something which makes you switch on the deep state of reflection even when you are amidst the chaos, but that will happen with time.

In the beginning, you do need a peaceful environment where you are not bothered time and again by anyone. If you live with a roommate or have several people in your household, either meditate at a time when nobody is around, or ask them to keep it quiet when you meditate.

Do Not Meditate on a Completely Empty Stomach

It is best not to meditate on a completely empty stomach because a rumbling tummy is likely to distract you every now and then during the practice. Meditate 2 hours after a meal, or a little before having one. If you feel extremely hungry right before meditation, eat something light.

Start Off Small

It is impressive to hear real-life examples of people who can meditate for hours. However, even expert monks weren't able to meditate for hours right when they started meditating.

Do not let such stories push you into trying something tough for you and then becoming demotivated when you find yourself unable to do it even for 5 minutes. The right way to go about this task is, to begin with just 2-minute meditation techniques or 5-minute ones and then slowly increase the duration.

CHAPTER 11

Mindful Meditative Practice and Simple Exercise Examples

In this chapter, we are going to go through the process of mindful meditation, and at the end, will provide simple examples of how to practice. These examples are meant to get your creative ideas flowing so that you are able to find what works best for you.

The key to overcoming suffering and finding that deep-rooted natural wisdom is through mindful meditation practice. Mindfulness is nurtured through sitting and meditating. While there are several types of meditative techniques that do involve sitting, some are meant to help us relax while others can produce an altered state of consciousness. Mindfulness is unique in that its intention is not to get us to change anything about ourselves. It is simply meant to make us more aware of what is going on from one moment to the next. Its purpose is to teach us to be present unconditionally no matter what is happening.

Sitting while practicing mindful meditation gives us the opportunity to be present at the moment just as we are. It gives us a glimpse of our inherent wisdom and helps to teach us how to stop the unnecessary suffering that occurs when we try to escape discomfort or pain. These are things we experience simply from being alive. Aches and pains are a part of life. We cannot fight it. We can, however, recognize those moments and use mindful meditation to get through them.

δ. Choose your environment. This step is key. You need to find a place where you will not be distracted. You will want to put any and all electronics away to avoid the temptation of social media. You will also want to be in a place where you will have no interruptions.

Sometimes, this can be difficult, especially if you have kids wanting to know if they can have a snack or when dinner will be. The place should be quiet and can be indoors or out depending on the weather. If you are lucky enough to live in an area that has warm weather year-round and you don't have neighbors who will ask what you are up to, go for it. Being close to nature is a very grounding feeling and helps in all meditative practices, even mindfulness. Once you find that place, you can detach yourself from the humdrum of everyday life. ***Side Note*** If you are attempting to cultivate your meditative practice, you might want to consider creating a space that is all your own and specifically dedicated to your meditation. In this space, you can have flowers, pictures, or inspirational items that help you to focus and can be a focal point.

ε. Get comfortable. You will need to be stationary for several minutes consecutively. That makes being comfortable particularly important. Make sure the temperature of the room is tolerable. While meditating, your body temperature may drop, so try to have a blanket nearby. You can sit on pillows or cushions...whatever you need to make that sitting position comfortable. You will also want to wear clothes that are comfortable. Sweat pants and a t-shirt are perfect.

φ. Set aside time. We've mentioned this before. Start out slow with ten to fifteen minutes per day. If you can do this in the morning and at night, perfect! If not, once per day is fine. It's a good idea to set a timer so that you aren't tempted to check the clock while you are practicing. You will want to have a soft buzz instead of a loud beeping or alarm. You don't want to be jarred out of your practice. That can be detrimental to all the relaxing meditation you just spent time on.

γ. Try different postures. There are some meditative techniques in which the practitioner can lie down. For mindful meditation, it is best to sit. You can cross your legs in the lotus position, stretch your legs out, or sit in a comfortable chair. Find what position you are most comfortable in and go with it. Again, there is no wrong way to meditate.

η. Quiet the mind. In the beginning, it might take a little more of your time to get your mind to quiet down and detach itself from everything you have going on in life. This can be difficult if you've had a particularly bad day. If you dwell on the events of the day, it can get the emotions stirred up. It is okay to take notice of that and then bring your focus back to meditative practice. In the beginning, you might feel a little awkward, and that is also okay. Once again, take note of the feeling and move on. Remember, this is for your overall wellbeing and psyche. It's good for you!

ι. Take several slow, deep breaths. Bring awareness to your breath. Take note of your inhales and exhales with each breath. Feel how the breath flows in and out of you, notice how it fills your lungs and releases through your mouth or nose. With each breath, make it longer than the last. Deep breathing helps your mind and body relax and prepares you to meditate mindfully. Noticing your breath is a practice in mindfulness all its own. You can observe your breath at any point in the day.

φ. You are not your thoughts. While you meditate, it is important to remind yourself that you are in control of the way you feel and the things you are thinking. When you take notice of your thoughts or emotions, you can recognize them and then put them back in their place so that you can focus on your practice and not your thoughts or emotions. Don't beat yourself up over those thoughts sneaking into your practice. It will happen from time to time. Acknowledge them and move on. **special note** Any time you are distracted from your practice, return to your breath as noted in step six.

κ. Focus on the present moment. Mindfulness meditation is about helping you to focus on the present. It is far too easy to let your mind wander and think about the past or the future. You can look at it this way. Your body is always in the present. It can't go back to the past or skip ahead to the future. Always try to focus on the present moment. Once again, when your mind or emotions wander, go back to your breath. That is what will grounded and bring you back to your reason for mindfully meditating.

Those are the steps that will get you into your meditative state. Once you are there, what happens is up to you. This is where things are different from one person to the next comes in. How you choose to take yourself through your practice is entirely up to you. Next, we are going to cover some mindful exercises that will help get you deeper into your meditations.

We've talked about how when the mind wanders; it's important to come back to your breath. Now, we are going to get into a little more detail with mindful breathing.

1. Take three easy, gentle breaths through your nose and exhale slowly and steadily. With each breath, feel your body slowing down and becoming immersed in your breaths.

2. Become fully aware of your breathing. With each exhale, take note of where in your body you feel the breath the most. It might be with the rise and fall of your chest. It may be through your nostrils as you exhale. Wherever it is, just take that moment to realize it where it is felt.

3. Now that you are aware of your exhales take note of your inhales. With each breath in, pay attention to any feelings of tension and note what it feels like as the breath enters your lungs.

4. Shift your awareness once more to your exhales. Observe the sound of your breath as it

leaves your body. There is no judgment, just observance.

5. Continue to breathe evenly and gently for several minutes.

6. Take note of what is happening inside your mind. If it is wandering or your thoughts are drifting, don't judge or criticize yourself. Notice, then redirect your attention back to your breaths.

7. After about ten minutes, open your eyes, and come back to your awareness. Notice your surroundings. Bask in the tranquility, peace, and stillness of the moment you just experienced.

As a beginner, this is a great exercise on awareness. It helps you to start to find your breaths, be aware of any thoughts that may sneak in, and get your focus back. Know and accept your mind for the wonderful thing that it is. We all have a tendency to let our mind wander. With practice, the breathing technique will become easier each day.

The next exercise we are going to practice is one in everyday mindfulness. This exercise is going to involve some of the things we do on a daily basis in which our autopilot takes over. We want to be mindful of everyday experiences, too. In doing so, we will be able to become better practitioners when it comes to mindful meditation.

This exercise is quite easy. Take some time to reflect on some of the activities you do during the week, but that is mindless in nature. Some good examples of these are; doing the dishes, brushing your teeth, walking the dog, driving to work, taking a shower or eating breakfast.

Over the next week, choose one of your daily, autopilot activities to focus on each day. There is nothing to be changed about your routine. Don't go slower or faster. Complete these activities as you always do. All you are doing now is increasing your level of awareness. Engage in one activity per day in a mindful manner. Don't rush through it; don't let your thoughts drift elsewhere. Perhaps while you walk the dog, take notice of your surroundings. What is the weather like? What does it smell like? What does the pavement feel like beneath your tennis shoes?

Once the week is over, write down your reactions to your experience. How did it feel to engage in a mindless activity mindfully? Was it any different than usual? You can do this again the next week with a different activity. Just remember, the point of this exercise is to be mindful in many of those activities that are considered mindless.

The next exercise we are going to talk about is mindfulness of the senses. This takes mindful breaths to the next level as it includes all of your senses. Just as we did with our breaths, we can use our other senses to deepen our meditation.

First, you will need to be in a comfortable, quiet place to sit. Make sure you have at least ten minutes, to begin with, but this is certainly an exercise that can be extended as time goes on. Sit down comfortably either on the ground or in a chair. With your back straight, relax your shoulders. You can either close your eyes or find something directly in front of you to focus your eyes.

- Begin with three gentle breaths in through the nose and exhale just as evenly as you inhaled. With each breath, feel your body slowing down and relaxing.

- Again, if your mind begins to wander, take note, and return your awareness to your breaths. (This is an important step in any meditative practice involving mindfulness. Never criticize your mind if it runs away. Simply bring it back to focus)

- Once you have your breathing under control, take note of the things you hear. The sound of your breath, or the sound of silence. Whatever you hear, notice them without judgment or any want for them to be something else.

- Next, take note of anything you might smell. You are only to take note of them. Don't try to figure out what they are. Let the scents come in through your nose and then let them pass without judgment.

- Now, focus on how your body feels as it sits on the floor or in the chair. Take note of the weight of your body. Be aware of the way your clothes feel against your skin, the temperature in the room. Take note of your hands and where they rest.

- Next, bring your awareness to the inside of your mouth. Is there anything you can taste? Whether it is something from earlier in the day or your lingering toothpaste, take note of it. If there is nothing that can be tasted, take note of that as well.

- If your eyes are closed, try to imagine what the room looks like. If it is somewhere you spend a lot of time; you might be familiar with where everything is in the room. What is on the walls? What is underneath you? What colors are the walls? Notice those and move on.

- Now, let's take note of what is happening inside your head. Are your thoughts going to the past or the future? If your mind is wandering, redirect your attention and bring everything back to your senses.

- After about ten minutes or so, come back to your surroundings. (This step is where a stopwatch will come in handy).

Our last exercise is going to be the mindful minute. While mindful meditation is something that should be done daily for around a half hour or so (once you get up to that, of course. Remember to start out small), there are times where life just gets in the way, and that's okay too. Some days, trying to find ten minutes is next to impossible. Everyone should be able to spare a minute, though, and that is what the mindful minute is about.

Our world is fast-paced and always on the move. That makes it hard to take some time to slow down and be in the moment. That can lead to stress, and once you feel stressed, it's a great time to take a minute to be mindful. Whether you are in your car or at the office, standing or sitting, this is something that you can do no matter where you are. All you need is one minute of quiet. If you are in the car, don't close your eyes. Anywhere else, feel free to do so. Stop whatever you are doing and then follow these steps:

1. Take note of your breath as it goes in through your nose, fills your lungs, and leaves your nose.

2. Use all of your senses to take note of what's happening around you. Feel the temperature of the room or outdoors, notice the smells, the sounds. Notice what the inside of your mouth tastes like.

3. Notice your emotions and thoughts that you are having at that very moment. Only notice

them. There is no judgment, no criticism, no emotion. You are detached from these thoughts and emotions.

4. If your mind drifts, bring it back to the moment and refocus on your breaths.

5. Open your eyes and come back to wherever you are.

Some of these steps are repeated from other methods of meditations mentioned earlier. The repetitive nature is what helps us to learn and memorize the process of mindful meditation. This practice will always begin by taking note of your breaths and end with opening your eyes and coming back to where you are. In every step, you want to notice everything. Be mindful of your senses, especially. Wandering thoughts are okay so long as you are able to come back to your moment. Mindful meditation is about finding that inner peace and connecting with people on a deeper level.

CHAPTER 13

Cultivating Mindfulness into daily life

Sustained practice of mindfulness is what brings the greatest results. To get them, you have to incorporate mindfulness and meditation as a habit in your day-to-day life. In this chapter, you will learn tips and tricks that can be used to develop a daily habit of mindfulness.

Tip #1: The Power of the Morning Ritual
Morning time is when your mind is the least cluttered with thoughts and emotions. Brain scans of various people have shown that the pre-frontal cortex of the brain, which is responsible for focus and attention, is most active just after waking up. This is because, during sleep, our memories and learnings are consolidated into the deeper neural network of our brain, which frees up the cortex for fresh processing.

So why not practice mindfulness when you are most likely to get the best results? Also, you are least distracted just after waking up. This is an advantage. As they say, if you win the morning, you win the whole day. So, it makes sense to set your day up for success by finishing off the mindfulness routine first thing in the morning.

Tip #2: Keep it Short and Sweet

The toughest part of building a habit is the initial phase where you struggle to change your state of mind from "I don't feel like doing it" to "I want to do it now." He who can motivate himself to do what is required will have the easiest time building the habit and also in life in general. This begs the question, "How do you go from not wanting to do it, to wanting to do it?" What makes us want to do something inherently boring and hard?

The answer lies in the question itself; we don't want to do anything boring and hard. So, if you can figure out a way to make it easy and exciting, you will have a better time developing the habit. Easy and Exciting – that's just another phrase for 'short and sweet.' And don't worry about whether you were able to achieve a

Zen-like state of pure consciousness while you practice it. Lower your expectations as much as possible. Redefine success as spending those five minutes in an attempt for mindfulness.

With this framework, you will feel success every day, and that leads to positive reinforcement for your brain, and you will start liking mindfulness more. And that leads to you practicing mindfulness more. And that leads to more positive reinforcement. So, it becomes a healthy, positive loop of actions and rewards whose outcome is a well-developed habit of mindfulness.

Tip #3: Create Effective Cues

Humans are creatures of habit. No matter how disciplined you are, without an effective system in place that helps you loop into the habit and track your progress, you will eventually fall out of the habit. So, it is important to have cues spread throughout your home and workplace to trigger you into the required state of mind. These cues can be anything from sticky notes and alarms to having a personal trainer or guide/mentor. Here are some examples of effective cues:

Time of the Day: You do not need to remind yourself to brush in the morning every day because, at an unconscious level, you have associated morning time with brushing teeth. So, start practicing mindfulness immediately after brushing your teeth in the morning, and it will become a habit set in stone because every day you will brush your teeth and that implies that every day you will practice mindfulness.

Calendar Notifications: This is pretty straightforward. Plan your days, weeks, and months on your calendar. Set specific deadlines and reminders. For example, you can have a reminder that pops up at 11.00 a.m., 4.00 p.m. and 9.00 p.m. every day that will remind you to practice the habit for five minutes. I have used this to develop good habits like drinking water, meditation, writing, exercise, etc.

Set Up Accountability: By informing your friends/family that you're taking up mindfulness as a daily habit, you set yourself up for social accountability which has been shown to be very effective in developing and maintaining habits. You will experience healthy social/peer pressure to practice the habit daily and also get cues that will keep you on your toes. The good thing about these clubs/groups is that everybody is on the same boat as you. Everyone wants to develop a mindfulness habit. So, it will be easier to find accountability buddies. In the worst-case scenario, you can just enforce a self-constraint that whenever you miss the five-minute mindfulness practice during the day, you will do ten push-ups. What this does is associate pain with not practicing mindfulness, so the next time you get a reminder, your brain will naturally be inclined towards doing the mindfulness activity instead of experiencing pain. Thank God for mental conditioning, eh?

Tip #4: Weave it into existing routines
The more you practice mindfulness, the better your mental health will become. So, you need to find every

excuse you can to practice mindfulness during the waking hours. Try to find a way to mix mindfulness with a pre-existing habit or routine like cooking, walking the dog, bathing, etc. Plus, you will be leveraging the existing mental framework associated with the old habit to form a new habit. Isn't that smart?

Tip #5: Cut Down Options

Decision-making sucks up your mental resources. If you wake up every day and debate with yourself on whether you need to do it or not, then you probably won't. You shouldn't have to decide. You should just fall into the process of it. For example, Barack Obama insisted that while he was in office, he would wear only black, blue, and gray suits. "I shouldn't have to decide on what I'm going to wear every day as I already have too many decisions to make for the country," he said.

In the best-seller Predictably Irrational, author Dan Ariely points out that keeping doors open prohibits us from taking action in a specific direction. So, he encourages people to close certain options voluntarily. This will supposedly help us de-paralyze ourselves in the process of decision-making and action-taking.

So, how can you apply this to mindfulness? Make sure that in your dedicated time slot for practicing mindfulness (create one if you haven't already), stay away from your mobile phone, social media, notifications, distractions, etc. This way, you can't be reminded of events that require your immediate attention. To develop a long-term habit of mindfulness, you need to let go of the short-term attention-seeking activities and events.

Conclusion

While many of the benefits of mindfulness meditation include physical changes to the body, it can be difficult to track them without scientific or medical help. Instead, the first positive changes that you are going to likely notice are going to include changes to the mental conditioning you have been subjected too for your entire life. Living in a modern society typically leads to a desire to hide our flaws from others as well as ourselves and to treat uncomfortable thoughts and feelings in much the same way. This, in turn, leads to a desire to revise the truth and rewrite personal histories until they show things in a more flattering light. While not necessarily the healthiest way to handle issues, this common cultural habit is actually an offshoot of the instinctual, primal desire towards flight or fight that help ancient humans avoid threats whether they were real or imaginary.

While it was this impulse that helped our ancient ancestors survive and thrive amongst harsh natural conditions, these days it is easy for it to instead lead to an undermining of the very traits and qualities that make us unique. This is perhaps mindfulness meditation's greatest benefit; it allows people to gain a deeper understanding of themselves which is the first step to a greater acceptance of both strengths and weakness and finding the best way to reconcile the two.

In place of this negative and potentially harmful mindset, regularly practicing mindfulness meditation can lead you to what is known as radical acceptance. Essentially it allows you to be more in touch with what you are experience and feeling at the moment without any of the negative filters imposed by society. Radical acceptance allows you to understand that just because you have the occasional negative thought or feeling doesn't mean that there is anything wrong with you, and it is an amazing and free experience. A significant part of radical acceptance is embracing all of your firsthand experiences as they are, something that learning to exist at the moment will make much more comfortable than it otherwise might be. Additionally, you will find that you will soon have a higher tolerance for negative experiences until you are ultimately able to let them occur without making them impact your overall mental state.

This improved mental state comes as a natural side effect of learning to be nonjudgmental not just of your thoughts but your experience as well. Cultivating mindfulness means leaning heavily on the suspension of inner, which is a result of putting greater thought into your feelings, thoughts, and reactions and why they make you feel the way they do.

Additionally, you will likely find that regularly practicing mindfulness meditation naturally improves your ability to be aware of your surroundings at all times, even when you feel otherwise occupied by specific thoughts or problems that you may be facing. Typically, most people are so focused on the mistakes they have made in the past or their plans for the future that they don't have any mental energy left over for the present. This is a precarious situation as it then becomes easy to miss out on all the pleasures of the present without even realizing what it is you are giving up in order to focus on the past which you cannot change or the future which is largely uncertain. Instead of existing in this mental fugue state, existing more frequently in the present allows you to strengthen your awareness of what is happening at any given moment, letting you take charge of your future in a more active way and banishing the specter of missed opportunities that so frequently hangs over the past.

This practice is what is known as meta-awareness, which is a state where you are able to interact with your thoughts and feelings in a more objective and detached way. This, in turn, allows you to more accurately measure your experiences to determine how they are affecting your sense of self without the baggage that such things typically carry around with them. Essentially, meta-awareness allows you to view yourself in a detached and objective manner which can benefit virtually every aspect of your life.

Lightning Source UK Ltd.
Milton Keynes UK
UKHW020625080121
376670UK00014B/1761